SLOGANS OR DISTINCTIVES

Reforming Christian Higher Education

David L. Wolfe

Harold Heie

UNIVERSITY
PRESS OF
AMERICA

Lanham • New York • London

Copyright © 1993 by
University Press of America®, Inc.
4720 Boston Way
Lanham, Maryland 20706

3 Henrietta Street
London WC2E 8LU England

Library of Congress Cataloging-in-Publication Data

Wolfe, David L.
Slogans or distinctives : reforming Christian higher education /
David L. Wolfe, Harold Heie.
p.   cm.
1. Church colleges—United States.   2. Educational change—United
States.   I. Heie, Harold, 1935– .   II. Title.
LC621.W65   1993   377'.8'0973—dc20   92–41860 CIP

ISBN 0–8191–8988–X (cloth : alk. paper)
ISBN 0–8191–8989–8 (pbk. : alk. paper)

The paper used in this publication meets the minimum requirements of
American National Standard for Information Sciences—Permanence
of Paper for Printed Library Materials, ANSI Z39.48–1984.

TO PAT AND JEAN

whose caring, patience,
encouragement and good humor
have sustained us.

PREFACE

Education is futuristic. It prepares people for a meaningful contribution to our common future. Christian liberal arts education, also futuristic, contributes to the development of the whole person. Consequentially, education that is Christian rests on an implicit theology of the human person, with curricula and community as common sources of learning. What we know is inextricably linked to what we do.

At Christian colleges, faculty members engage students in understanding relationships between faith and culture, between the church and the world, between the Kingdom of God and the realm and rule of sin. While many educators have accepted Niebuhr's description of Christian faith as "Christ against culture," Christian education seeks to penetrate culture with an incarnational faith. The Christian colleges' quest for excellence includes the dimensions of equity, justice, integrity, faith, love and shalom. The goal of Christian educators is the preparation of a people who will bring enriching values to the world, who will be a presence for Christ in society. Since we are disciples of Christ, our Lord is our starting point in all learning.

In this stimulating work, Wolfe and Heie call us to the exciting enterprise of Christian education. This means moving beyond fragmentation and beyond simplistic piety to actually engaging integrative studies at a scholarly level. On behalf of the 84 member institutions of the Christian College Coalition, I applaud the authors' emphasis and commend their work. Education can best serve our world when it complements the pluralism of our time by decisively teaching from a Christian world view and doing so with a steadfast commitment to scholarly excellence.

Wolfe and Heie do us a special service by their positive approach, their practical illustrations and their constructive stimulus for innovation. Their work is especially timely because they emphasize faith/learning integration and Christian social responsibility which calls administrators, faculty and students to join in innovations that will enhance the effectiveness and relevance of Christian higher education. As we work together at racial and ethnic diversity, at economic and environmental issues, at national and global responsibilities, we may find the Christian college is at its best in addressing such concerns creatively.

As we look to the future of Christian higher education, we of the Christian College Coalition staff are grateful for the privilege of helping with the publication and promotion of this book. This work may well help to keep open the American mind.

Dr. Myron S. Augsburger
President
Christian College Coalition

TABLE OF CONTENTS

FOREWORD

This is not the first contribution that Wolfe and Heie have made to the literature on Christianity and higher education. In 1987, they published *The Reality of Christian Learning*, a collection of original essays and responses by Christian scholars on the integration of faith and learning in seven academic disciplines. Introduced by a programmatic essay about different approaches to integration, and concluding with a retrospective piece, it demonstrated a level of intellectual maturity that Christian colleges (and Christian scholars in any setting) would do well to emulate. It stands miles beyond the applications and polemics that used to pass for integration, not to mention simplistic spiritualizing tacked onto a positivist epistemology. Fundamental philosophical and theological issues inherent in the disciplines are addressed with a constructive rather than defensive spirit.

In the present volume they bring that same mature perspective to bear on Christian higher education itself, calling for a return to those priorities that should make Christian colleges distinctive. Our colleges are strong on slogans (i.e., on "P.R."), but Wolfe and Heie unpack the slogans, uncovering neglected educational objectives and setting a new agenda for a fully ordered Christian higher education.

Their objectives, which have to do with a community of mentors and apprentices committed to a Christian world view, will be applauded by most readers. It is the agenda which follows that will raise eyebrows and elicit charges about "dreamers," for after surveying innovations already in operation and finding them wanting, they set out far-reaching proposals for faculty development, faculty-student relations, and curricular change, capping it off with an "Ambrose House" model for outstanding students who are the Christian scholars and faculty of the future.

The problem is how to break the vicious cycle. We draw faculty from graduate universities who are unprepared to deal with integrative studies; the students they produce are therefore ill-prepared too; yet they in their turn become scholars and teachers, and the cycle of inadequacy continues. The proposal presented here is intended to break the cycle, to provide for the future a stream of scholars who have done extensive, rigorous, individualized work in theology, intellectual history, and philosophical foundations, who have learned to think as Christians in their disciplines and about life and learning as a whole.

Nor are student development and co-curricular activities to be neglected. Rather they are to become an integral part of education, instead of being regarded as diversions into "real life"—and as is often the case, educationally counterproductive.

I heartily applaud.

One might question whether the present scene is as discouraging as might seem to be implied. I think, for instance, of a recent program for faculty and curricular development funded by The Pew Charitable Trusts through the Christian College Consortium, running for six years and producing sustained emphases and institutionalized outcomes. "Ethics Across the Curriculum," with which I am most familiar, provided a feast of faculty workshops and research leading to new or improved ethics courses and course components potentially in every department of participating colleges. It is still spotty and insufficient, but it offers an encouraging model for sustained in-service training coordinated by an institutional task force with a college-wide mandate, a model that could well be copied.

The frequent cry is that we are too busy already, and the smaller the college the more difficult it is to find time to plan and execute such developmental tasks. The time problem haunts and frustrates us everywhere, with our typical undergraduate teaching loads plus committee assignments plus student advising, not to mention outside professional tasks and family and church and community responsibilities and all the dean wants us to do. Changing trends in higher education generally keep us busy anyway, what with outcomes statements and devising new evaluation techniques, and preparing for accreditation visits and departmental evaluations. So many who read this book are likely to sigh with sheer frustration. And of course there is the money problem touched on at the end. All education proposals have price tags.

Yet Wolfe and Heie rightly respond that it is a question of priorities. What is distinctive about the idea of a Christian college anyway? Is it not the integration of faith and learning? Allan Bloom complains in *The Closing of the American Mind* about the value relativism of today's students, about their loss of any world view to ground values in reality and about their lacking any ideal of the person one should become. This sounds like an open invitation to the Christian college, for Bloom's concerns are at the heart of what integration is about as well as, in his estimation, the heart of higher education generally. Wolfe and Heie are right: it **is** a question of priorities. Their book simply must be read and discussed, its proposals evaluated, probably modified and adapted too. For amidst today's surge of voices, their vision calls us back to basics, and forward to our *raison d'etre*.

Arthur F. Holmes
Wheaton College

TO THE READER

Sometimes books yet unborn cry out to be written. The voices by which the present book cried out were those of our own experiences and the experiences of many colleagues past and present. The ideas, arguments and criticisms in this volume have been voiced in our presence by innumerable Christian scholars and teachers who follow the vision of Christian higher education. Often these women and men were in positions too sensitive or too powerless to raise their voices effectively. Sometimes the authors were they. Perhaps this book will in some small way speak for their dream and the educational priorities which it requires.

Many of the substantive issues we raise, especially those of faith-learning integration and of Christian social responsibility in education have been addressed in their own right more fully elsewhere. Some of that literature has been listed at the end of chapter 1. Our concern is with the way in which those issues intersect with the educational structures, priorities and programs of existing Christian higher education. This is a book about how and why current Christian colleges have serious problems dealing with those issues effectively.

This book, however, may serve more than one purpose. Its intended audiences are those involved in Christian higher education, namely administrators, teachers and students. It may also be of considerable value to those on the outside of the enterprise who wish to get an idea of what a Christian college might be. These readers may include prospective Christian college students, as well as educators who are curious about the distinctives of Christian higher education. The chapter on innovations in Christian higher education may also be of help to Christian students who wish to explore currently available alternatives to the standard college program, or to college graduates who wish to undertake an investigation of faith and learning issues at the graduate level.

We have written this book as loyal critics of existing Christian college priorities. Between us we have served over half a century in those colleges as student, teachers and administrator. Nothing said here should be understood as critical of the ideal of Christian higher education, though its particular embodiments often betray that ideal. We have not hesitated to say that this is so .

The constituency of Christian colleges (students, parents, pastors and donors) upon whom the colleges depend financially often have a very constricted vision of what Christian education is all about. This, along with a residual fear of thinking and learning on the part of many in these groups, acts as a major hobble to creativity in Christian higher education. We have not pretended to deal with the constituency issue, except in passing. It is, perhaps, the voice of another book yet unborn crying out to be written, but not, we hope, by us.

We wish to thank our colleagues over the years, whose voices we attempt to articulate in these pages, for their commitment and stimulus. None of them are, of course, responsible for any transgressions of fact or taste that we may have unintentionally perpetrated. We especially appreciate the encouragement of Arthur Holmes and Stan Gaede at various stages in this writing project. We also express our thanks to the Christian College Coalition for its commitment to disseminating this work, and to the Lilly Endowment for making this possible through a generous grant to the Christian College Coalition devoted to the goal of enhancing the College Development programs at the various Coalition colleges. In particular, Rebekah Burch Basinger, Myron Augsburger and Karen Longman were the Coalition leaders who made this dissemination possible. We extend our deep appreciation for their efforts on our behalf. We also extend a special thank you to Beth De Leeuw and Shirley Groff for their indispensable work far beyond the call of duty in caring for those jobs in the production of this book which were not half so much fun as writing it.

... At Milan I came to Bishop Ambrose, who had a worldwide reputation, was a devout servant of yours and a man whose eloquence in those days gave abundantly to *Thy people the fatness of Thy wheat, the gladness of Thy oil and the sober intoxication of Thy wine*. Though I did not realize it, I was led to him by you so that, with full realization, I might be led to you by him. That man of God welcomed me as a father and, in his capacity of bishop, was kind enough to approve of my coming there. I began to love him at first not as a teacher of the truth (for I had quite despaired of finding it in your Church) but simply as a man who was kind and generous to me. . . . I hung intently on his words, but I was not interested in what he was really saying and stood aside from this in contempt. I was much pleased by the charm of his style, which, although it was more learned, was still, so far as the manner of delivery was concerned, not so warm and winning as the style of Faustus. With regard to the actual matter there was, of course, no comparison. Faustus was merely roving around among Manichaean fallacies, while Ambrose was healthily teaching salvation. But salvation is far from sinners of the kind that I was then. Yet, though I did not realize it, I was drawing gradually nearer.

Augustine
The Confessions

PROLOGUE: A RABBIT TALE

The following story is certified true by a county court clerk (it happened to his cousin) and the Vermont side judge who related it to me.

As happens so often, the neighbors of many years were not on the best of terms. Truth to tell they got along very badly. The current problem of a long history of problems was **her** dog and **their** rabbit.

Her dog wanted to get at their rabbit in the worst way. Since the dog was usually kept indoors or on a tether its desire was impotent; when it did get loose on occasion the rabbit cage frustrated its eager instincts. Such occasions, however, did little to improve relations between the neighbors. "That filthy beast of yours is over here after our rabbit again! Keep him tied up or I'll have him shot, so help me."

So it was with a very special horror that she came to the screen door on that fateful morning to discover her dog on the outside looking in. He was covered with dirt and carried firmly and proudly clutched in his jaws the limp body of their rabbit. The scenario of the rabbit's demise instantly flashed onto the screen of her fevered imagination: the break from his tether, the dash to the neighbor's rabbit cage, the eager assault on the cage, the decision to dig, the panic-stricken rabbit, the breach of the cage, the lunge.

She was so overwhelmed by the implications of the dead rabbit for future relations with her neighbor that she momentarily forgot to be angry with the dog, though it crossed her mind that they would probably bring pressure to have him put away for being dangerous. She was thinking rapidly and not too clearly.

Then like a crystalline revelation, calm and pure, she saw what she must do. Prying the dirt-encrusted body of the rabbit from the jaws of her dog, she carried it to the bathroom. Laying it gently in the bathtub, she sponged the soil from its fur and examined it for visible damage. To her satisfaction there were no signs of violence. The head hung limply, but there were no wounds. Evidently her dog had broken the small animal's neck, but had not yet gnawed on the body.

Now she was working with the methodical calmness of a practiced criminal carrying out a routine operation. She shampooed the rabbit's fur, blow dried it to the fluffiness of a new stuffed animal, cleaned the dirt from the corners of its eyes with a Q-tip, toothbrushed its ears until they were smooth and pink, and generally restored the rabbit to its original condition or better.

Admiring her meticulous job of restoration, she contemplated the next step in her plan. It was the riskier undertaking. She knew that the neighbors were away for a few days, but she did not know exactly how long they were to be gone. Perhaps they were home already. No, by now they would be over here screaming at her about the rabbit. She looked out the window. Their car was not in the driveway.

Gathering the small, dead creature up in her hands she walked to the door. Cautiously she peered out. It was still early; no one was about. Trying to appear businesslike, she walked briskly across the yard, into the neighbor's yard and over to the rabbit cage. Without stopping to examine all of the details, she opened the door of the cage and slipped the rabbit inside. For just a moment she thought to herself, "How natural he looks." Then she closed the cage door and quickly slipped away.

She passed the time by bathing the dog and compulsively removing every trace of the rabbit's presence from her home. So later in the day when she heard the neighbors' car doors slam, she was somewhat surprised to discover how tense she was. Only moments later there came a bloodcurdling shriek of an intensity for which she was completely unprepared.

It seems that the poor rabbit had died of natural causes just before the neighbors had left on their trip and they had given it a decent burial.

* * *

As in the tragicomic rabbit tale, we in Christian higher education are forever digging up our well-used slogans, shampooing and blow drying them, cleaning the dirt from the corners of their eyes and trying to restore them to a place of prominence.

Looked at from one point of view the present volume is just such a piece of rabbit cleaning. It calls for a return to the priorities that should make Christian colleges distinctive. On the other hand it advances the claim that we are so seldom in a position to take our slogans seriously, that to do so is virtually to set a whole new agenda for Christian higher education.

Here we make a series of proposals. We are under no illusions about their shortcomings. Neither the proposals nor the criticisms of the existing structures that give rise to them are laid out in exhaustive detail. Neither is there any particular pretense to originality, though originality is not denied should it prove to be the case. Our concern is to stimulate dialogue, insight and educational action.

Some of our slogans have been around in the rabbit cage of our literature for so long that they would probably prove to be truly shocking if we were to take their meaning seriously. One of the slogans not dealt with in this volume, but which is often encountered, is that our education is "Christ-centered." We strongly suspect that, like so many cliches, a serious application of this slogan would revolutionize our educational lives. But, as is so often said, that is a topic for another occasion.

We have tried to examine the significance and explore the implications of some of the specifically educational slogans currently in the catalogs and public relations literature of Christian colleges. We hope that what we have done will prove stimulating and provocative both to those who are inside as well as those who are skeptical about the enterprise of Christian higher education.

The pages which follow may become the basis for discussions among Christian college professionals, both administrators and faculty. Christian students considering college work may find both an articulation of what Christian higher education is and might be, as well as a survey of alternatives to traditional programs. Perhaps it may also serve as an introduction to what genuine Christian academia aspires to be, for those who know it only in caricature. Finally, these pages may inspire Christian lay people, who expect much of their colleges, to insist that they become the special Christian mission they claim to be and then to support them with their offspring and money.

Christian liberal arts colleges of the familiar type have been around for a long time now, some for more than a century. Most are loaded with talent and sacrifice. Some also have excellent resources. They are also abundantly stocked with rhetoric and slogans about their mission. They deserve more than Q-tips and blow drying.

CHAPTER 1

FROM SLOGANS TO DISTINCTIVES

The Slogans of Christian Higher Education

"It's the real thing!" "Give me liberty or give me death." "Speak softly, but carry a big stick." "Better dead than Red." "Education for democratic citizenship."

All of these are slogans that were designed for arousing interest, inciting enthusiasm, engendering loyalty or achieving a unity of feeling and spirit. Some writers have called those emotive functions the ceremonial uses of slogans. For most colleges the Latin or Greek mottoes on their institutional crests are of purely ceremonial significance. Were you to translate the motto into English it would have little relevance to the institution's educational policy and practice. For most institutions what does a slogan like *Lux et veritas* mean? Its function is simply social and emotional.

And yet, we must not underestimate the importance of catchy wording in articulating our political, commercial, and educational enterprises. Think, for a moment, of the advantage in appeal of "developing the leadership potential of American youth" over "I.Q.-segregated training program for future military executives."

Nevertheless, some slogans do indeed have non-ceremonial uses. In this they wed emotional appeal to a set of possible assertions, definitions and/or proposals for action. The problem and promise of a slogan is its rich ambiguity. At worst the ambiguity of a slogan permits it to degenerate easily into an empty catch phrase. At best, however, the ambiguity of a slogan permits it to imply a rich and complex set of activities and goals. As in politics and advertising, slogans have played an important role in educational thought. In fact, the importance of slogans in education has led some to state that "a philosophy of education is literally a **system** of slogans. It is indeed the apex of educational sloganizing."

However, given the ambiguity of educational slogans, we must be careful to pin down, at least to some extent, the educational proposals they intend to prescribe. The importance of interpreting a slogan by specifying the range of activities it proposes leads the same writers to offer us the following rules for slogan use:

> **When trying to find the meaning of a slogan, seek its interpretation.** Corollary: **Never use a slogan in such a way that you encourage asking for its meaning without being prepared to offer an interpretation.** Corollary: **Do not change interpretations without giving clear, and preferably prior, notice.** (Emphasis is in the original.)

Having been careful to point out that "slogan" is not necessarily a derogatory term, especially when we have interpreted our slogans (and the sub-slogans that our broader slogans imply), they continue: "In a well-constructed philosophy of education we find not only interpretations given for sub-slogans, we find also more general slogans which encompass the sub-slogans and give to the whole scheme an inner consistency and an outward charm."

So "slogan" is not necessarily a bad word. Slogans can accomplish a great deal that abstract prose cannot. We should not hesitate, then, to admit that the Christian educational community has used slogans, just as all other educational communities. The real danger in slogans is that we may forget the substance for which the slogans stand. When this happens, they degenerate to mere public relations tools — recruiting placards for students and susceptible teachers.

Let us see then, what substance may lie behind the principal slogans of Christian higher education. If we go hunting for educational slogans, it will not take us very long to spot our prey. A quick scanning of the history-and-philosophy-of-the-college section — those few pages near the front — of a couple of Christian college catalogs will give a generous list. Here are some of the slogan expressions you are very apt to encounter in your brief examination. See if these look familiar.

"All truth is God's truth"
"Integration of faith and learning"
"Holistic education" (or "education of the whole person")
"Christian leadership development"
"The personal touch"

If the slogans or slogan fragments you find are not these exact ones, they are probably very close equivalents.

Since it is all too easy to allow slogans like these to have a merely ceremonial function, it is all the more important for those who are serious about the enterprise of Christian higher education to attempt an interpretation of these slogans into the proposals they suggest. It is our point of view that such interpretation is not only necessary and possible, but that it will also reveal that these slogans have illuminating inner connections, forming a "slogan system" that has not only integrity and insight, but attractiveness and charm.

(1) All Truth Is God's Truth

Evangelical Christians begin with a predisposition to believe that Scripture is a place where truth is to be found. Depending upon the historical tradition in which they stand, they may feel that beyond biblical exegesis it is desirable to systematize, elaborate and apply biblical insights in theological formulations. For some Christians theology is the outer rim of the Christian's permitted intellectual activity. To venture farther away from the hub of biblical revelation is to risk being thrown off the wheel into the abyss of unbelief by the centrifugal force of human intellectual pride.

Now there is no denying that human intellectual achievements in the various academic disciplines are often founded upon values and assumptions that are antagonistic to a Christian perspective. This does create complexities and tensions when those disciplines are entered into by Christian scholars. Nevertheless, it is a profoundly Christian assumption that God has been active, not only redemptively in the history of Israel and the life, death and resurrection of Jesus Christ, but also in nature, human life and history, and even in the cultural productions of human beings in all times and places. Furthermore, while Scripture reveals God's purposes and redemptive actions on our behalf, it by no means degrades the significance of Scripture to observe that not all that God intended us to know is contained in those writings. Unless, of course, God did not intend for us to know the causes of disease, the use of moveable type to print Bibles, or the telephone number of the local poison control center. Christian higher education proceeds on the premise that it is proper for the Christian scholar to regard **the exploration, not just of biblical and theological understanding, but of all disciplines as a legitimate investigation of God's activity.**[1] All truth, wherever encountered or by whom uttered, is God's truth made available to us. These insights do not replace biblical and theological insights, but become part of a whole picture of life and the world.

(2) Integration of Faith and Learning

Illustrations and devotional applications are often drawn from the various academic disciplines by preachers and theological instructors. Such illustrations rarely have any intimate relation to the actual doing of the discipline in question; they remain essentially outside the discipline. Retelling an historical incident in a sermon may be edifying, but it is a long way from doing critical history.

The word "integration" is related to the words "integral" and "integrity." Two items form an **integral whole** if together they become one, unified new item. A complex item has **integrity** if it holds together (remains unified) under stress. Two areas of concern, such as one's religious faith commitment and pursuing an academic discipline, may be brought into an integral whole, into a complex, unified view of reality insofar as they share at least some common concerns and assumptions.

---

[1]Reference to these clarified slogans (or goals), when they occur later in this book, will usually take some shortened but recognizable form. For example, this one will be "exploring knowledge across disciplines." In each reference the full meaning of the slogan is intended even if not articulated.

This "integral" approach to relating faith and learning presupposes that the dedicated Christian scholar is operating **within** the academic discipline and is willing to submit to the rules essential to participating in that discipline, despite the tensions this may raise for her either as a Christian or as an academician.

The goal of this attempt may simply be to become a Christian psychologist, Christian philosopher, Christian economist or whatever. But in the long run, a community of Christian academicians and students in dialogue may hope to **develop a unifying conceptual framework informed by Christian ideas for interpreting and acting in the world,**[2] including thinking and operating in all of the academic disciplines. This is commonly referred to as **developing a Christian world and life view.** This is the cognitive goal **par excellence** of Christian higher education. The cognitive dimension of human existence is not everything, however.

(3) Holistic Education

In some Christian circles understanding is clearly subordinated to evangelistic fervor or emotional worship. But even when intellectual activity is regarded as of first importance, no Christian tradition regards it as eliminating the importance of worshiping or service; at most it is given the status of *primus inter pares* ("first among equals").

Because the Christian view of the human person is decisively **not** that we are disembodied intellects, Christian education does not indulge in the luxury of giving the intellectual side of human beings **exclusive** attention. Such an educational approach is artificial in any case. What we perceive and understand reflects what we care about. Similarly, our perceptions and understandings guide our actions and caring. We are complex beings, embodied centers of creative, caring awareness.

Having said all this, education, especially higher education, is eminently characterized by its critical, self-reflective component. For this rea-

---

[2]Hereafter this is referred to as "developing an integrated Christian framework."

son, if education is not to be thoughtless indoctrination or verbal response training, it must emphasize this reflective aspect of the cognitive attitude.

Christians in higher education, therefore, may regard the affective, the religious and the practical as parts of their bailiwick, but always provided they **emphasize the development of abilities and capacities such as caring, feeling, acting, worshiping and serving in relation to the goal of developing cognitive abilities.**[3] Christian higher education is an attempt to address the whole person, albeit from a cognitive perspective. This is what, among other things, distinguishes a college from a church or a health spa.

(4) Christian Leadership Development

Caring for what we observe through the lenses of a carefully examined Christian world and life view constitutes one of the goals of Christian higher education mentioned earlier. What we see when we look at the world is a staggering proliferation of needs and problems. We see a world which needs food more than catchy commercial jingles, medical attention more than novel clothing styles, freedom and justice for the oppressed more than a new deodorant, reconciliation and peace more than better graphics in its video games.

We also see a church which too often has arranged its priorities in alignment with the secular culture. All too frequently electronic glitz and high powered institutional programs are substituted for the caring community that sacrificially sets aside its own luxuries and petty prejudices to express Christ's love, even to people far away.

This is not the place for a catalog of the ills of the world or the dirty laundry of the church. Not all of the world is ill, but even its best parts need help to become excellent. Not all of the church's laundry is dirty, but even redeemed humanity needs all the help it can get to love creatively and well.

The point is this. Because higher education is **about** something — sets its sights on a world, with the accompanying complexities and problems — it is an opportunity to move a caring individual to service. Christian higher

---

[3]The brief version of this will be "non-cognitive development."

education has as one of its goals the **development of a special sense of responsibility for the use of knowledge, skills and abilities in addressing the needs and problems facing the church and the world**[4] — the development of Christian leadership in local, national and global settings.

In this connection another slogan sometimes encountered is that Christian education is for "faith, learning **and living**." The meaning behind this slogan gains its force both from the fact that human beings are not just believing and thinking beings; they must **live and act** (the holistic emphasis) and from the present goal ("addressing human needs") in its emphasis upon caring service and responsibility. "Praxis" is an expression commonly used to refer to the lived, practical action aspect of human existence. Sometimes it specifically refers to action that is consciously guided by theory. The underlined portion of the expression "... **and living**," as well as goals three and four give a strong emphasis on **praxis** to Christian higher education. Such education is **engaged** education; distinctions sometimes made among head, heart and hand have no ultimate dominion over Christian education. The biblical concept of truth clearly includes not just gaining knowledge, but also "living the truth." (See III John 3.)

(5) **The Personal Touch**

Human beings are always, most naturally and predominantly, social beings — members of communities. Our values, taken-for-granted habits, expectations, and as sociologists have forcefully pointed out, even our beliefs reflect our social relationships.

Throughout our lives we are initiated into new stages of human activities through our membership in groups and our relationships to mentors and peers in those groups. Our parents initiate us into fundamental human customs, language and constraints as family members. Our elementary school teachers and peers initiate us into institutional rule observance, problem solving, written language, computation, frustration tolerance and delay of biological gratification. Our high school teachers and peers initiate us into the basic rules of self-government, academic self-discipline and appreciation of the varieties of human knowledge and achievement.

---

[4] We will refer to this as the goal of "addressing human needs."

College, too, is a time of initiation, but not just an extension of high school. In high school our teachers may try to teach us, say, the facts of history and science. In college we are initiated into the doing of (or at least an appreciation of doing) history and science by teachers who are themselves qualified scholars. This is a **qualitative** jump. It demands that students be able to observe first-hand the doing of an academic discipline by mentors and older peers. It involves the sometimes subliminal acquisition of perceptions, values, assumptions and methods of scholarly activity in general and in particular disciplines. It further involves acquiring a certain set of virtues that characterize a working scholar, such as creative curiosity, intellectual honesty and openness to critical dialogue with the scholarly community. It also means acquiring a vision of the inner structure of a discipline, its significance for life and the world, and, for a Christian, its place within a Christian world and life view.

Ideally a Christian college **attempts to optimize relationships within a learning community as the context for pursuing the other goals, especially for promoting academic initiation through individual relationships between mentors and students.**[5] Discipling has always been an important feature of Christian education. **The personal touch** between mentor and apprentice is no less important in Christian higher education.

Tacit Assumptions About Christian Higher Education

College catalogs, recruiting brochures, books about Christian higher education and lectures on Christian educational distinctives all may make claims based on the goals we have discussed in this chapter. These are the **explicit goals** of Christian higher education. Beyond these explicit goals, however, there lie a number of other goals. These further expectations may not even be consciously formulated or articulated by educators, parents or students who are reflecting on Christian colleges. Nevertheless, parents, students and sometimes (but less often) college teachers and administrators may think of Christian education as implying these goals. Let us call these the **tacit goals** or **implicit assumptions** about Christian higher education.

---

[5]In future references this is simply called "initiation through mentor/student relationships."

Often these tacit goals are of a highly personal nature. For example, some of the older Christian colleges set great stock in photographing second, third, fourth and fifth generation students, offspring from families who have unbroken histories of attending the college. The goal of maintaining and recognizing prestige dynasties of alumni is hardly an explicit goal or important educational priority of higher education, though of course there are some groups of persons who have strong feelings about this.

Family traditions aside, some expectations about Christian colleges are very widely accepted. Some of these are the sorts of things one might hope for when young persons join any community of their peers, such as the establishing of significant friendships and the finding of a marriage partner. Nevertheless, college goals of friendship and marriage have a special significance among Christians. The reason for this is the particular preferences, expectations and moral constraints among Christians that favor marriage to those having a common faith. A non-Christian may find a mate at a singles' bar or in the classified ads, but Christians are typically more selective. In this sense, the Christian college does play an important role in the lives of young Christians. Something quite similar may be said about the role of the Christian college community in founding life-time friendships grounded in a common faith. Sometimes these friendships become significant sources of ideas, personal mobility and of change within the broader Christian community.

Perhaps even more important to many parents and students are the specifically protectionist religious expectations which are held concerning Christian higher education. The environment of Christian scholars, both mature and novitiate, is assumed to provide a "safe" situation for students to spend four years at a formative time in their lives. It is thought to guarantee the preservation of the student's commitment in general and orthodox evangelical faith in particular. There is, of course, some point to the notion that membership in a group which shares one's assumptions and beliefs gives a greater sense of plausibility to those beliefs. Socially shared beliefs are harder to doubt, all things being equal.

The problem with this last set of tacit goals — a guarantee of the student's faith and orthodoxy — is that all things are not equal in an educational context. This is especially true of those things which insulate beliefs and keep them safe from questioning. Genuine higher education, and this is true of Christian higher education, requires the freedom to question, to critically examine alternative claims to knowledge and to require reasons for what one believes.   Higher education which fails to grant this freedom to students, indeed which fails to force students to face these issues, fails **as education.** While these critical aspects of education are not **distinctively Christian, they are legitimately part of what a Christian college is all about as a college.** In this sense, while a Christian context encourages belief, it does not guarantee it. A Christian college community is **not** the safest place for believers, but it ought to be a good place for believers to mature intellectually.

Career Education

One widespread goal of **recent** Christian higher education is career preparation. We should hasten to add some qualifiers here. Much of Christian education in the past **has** been oriented to immediate career application. For example many three-year Bible institute programs prepared students for missionary service or the pastorate. As the level of paranoia about intellectual matters subsided in the American evangelical community, it was seen that such three-year specialized programs were inadequate as **higher education.** They did not prepare Christians to communicate with the broader culture and address its needs. There were also specifically job-oriented or technical Christian schools in areas like engineering, but they did not pretend to be the sort of school that accomplishes the distinctive goals Christian liberal arts colleges espoused.

It appears that the need for specialized training as a prerequisite for entering the job market has had its effect on the college curriculum. Earlier generations of students could go from a liberal arts program directly into the marketplace almost regardless of their majors, unless they aspired to a profession or ministry that required postgraduate study. Business did not require an undergraduate degree in business administration; there was no such thing as computer science; undergraduate programs in the service professions such as social work were unknown. Students graduated with majors in history, philosophy or literature and went to work as entrepeneurs, teachers, journalists, executives or farmers; or they went on to medical school, graduate engineering programs or theological seminary, to cite some instances.

Now specialized training, along with externally imposed professional standards, have become increasingly part of undergraduate liberal arts programs, in Christian colleges as well as elsewhere. It is **in this sense** that career preparation is a recent tacit goal of Christian higher education. Only recently do we expect a liberal arts undergraduate degree to represent sufficient technical training to make a student competitive in a specialized job market. In the past a liberal arts education was often regarded as a broadly humanizing preparation for a productive life. For the Christian this had a distinctive significance.

The impact, positive and negative, of these developments will be discussed later. Nevertheless, such career preparation goals are secondary when compared with the **distinctive** goals of Christian higher education. This is especially true because such specialized programs compete for the limited economic and curricular resources of the Christian college. Without any other considerations entering in, Christian colleges must be most careful to be sure their distinctive emphases receive unquestioned priority in funding. They must rigorously assess career-oriented programs for their possible economic impact upon the distinctive components of the total program.

So the tacit goals and expectations that are often imposed on Christian higher education, but rarely officially espoused, get a mixed review. To some extent these tacit goals have merit. In the case of the specifically religious goals there is ambiguity. To some extent these goals may tend to confuse the college with a church.[6]

Yet in all cases, whether or not the tacit goals are reasonable, **they are not distinctive goals for Christian higher education**. At best they appear to be by-products of valid educational goals relating to social and cognitive maturity, but they are not goals which the Christian college should institutionally try to guarantee.

---

[6]See the Notes on Chapter 1.

Christian Educational Distinctives

What, then, are the **distinctive** features of Christian higher education? There are some tacit expectations which may or may not be distinctively Christian. These would include finding a Christian mate and protecting personal faith. Such goals or expectations are **not essentially educational,** and so are not among the distinctive features of Christian higher education.

Other objectives of Christian higher education are features common to all higher education. This would include such things as creative and critical thinking, understanding one's cultural legacy, in-depth grasp of some discipline or skill area and the ability to write reasonably complex, coherent English. These goals, while clearly educational and appropriate to the Christian college, are **not distinctives** of Christian higher education.

The **distinctive** features of Christian higher education are established by the slogans which it uses. Our interpretation and analysis of those slogans strongly suggest that aside from being an educational institution in the fullest sense, a Christian college is a community of mentors and their apprentices committed to exploring with rigorous intellectual honesty God's activity in all areas of nature, history, society and culture. This community is committed to developing a Christian unifying interpretive framework in which all the disciplines and their results are viewed in a comprehensive way. Finally, while placing priority on cognitive development, such development is regarded as properly inseparable from affective and behavioral development (e.g., caring, worshiping, serving); such attention to the whole range of personal and social development requires that the academic community cannot carry out its cognitive goals without being a caring, serving community which is involved in celebrating humanity's joys and identifying with its needs and problems. This serving grows out of a Christian world and life view, and in turn conditions the structure and content of the scholarship that contributes to the formation of that world and life view.

Perhaps an example would be helpful. Because human beings have a pivotal place in God's creation and because of our particular interests in and obligations toward them, it is imperative to understand their nature and role in an adequate comprehensive world and life view. This requires that many forms of inquiry be employed, including theological, anthropological, sociological, psychological, linguistic and biological. To carry out this study requires a community of scholars who are specialists, but willing to trust and listen to each other. They must also initiate (as only scholarly mentors can) junior scholars into this open-ended enterprise of understanding the human person. At any point in our study, what understanding we have should lead us to appreciate and wonder at the mysteries and complexity of God's work, but also to see paths of service in improving medical care, psychological therapy, learning, teaching and social change. Experience in the disciplines and in service may lead to new insights and areas of investigation that in turn may modify the whole structure of our belief system. This could happen, for instance, when a psychologist working with children who have learning problems sees language acquisition in a new way that suggests a whole new theory about the nature and function of language. At this point the circle is complete and practical action feeds academic theorizing, research and world view construction just as such cognitive endeavors suggest applications in the world of experience.

In short, the five goals are united by meaningful internal connections: God has acted in all aspects of creation. A community of learners has assembled to weave a rich tapestry of insights from the various disciplines to help them understand, appreciate and serve in response to God's actions. Each goal either grounds or is grounded in the other goals.

This chapter describes the Christian college ideal. Is there such a community?

NOTES ON CHAPTER 1

On Slogans

References in this chapter, including the quotations, to the analysis of slogans and slogan systems are to "The Logic of Slogans" by B. Paul Komisar and James E. McClellan which is found on pages 195-214 in *Language and Concepts in Education*, edited by B. Othanel Smith and Robert H. Ennis (Chicago: Rand McNally, 1961).

On Faith-Learning Issues

New literature is constantly appearing in this area. Among recent publications are *The Reality of Christian Learning* edited by Harold Heie and David L. Wolfe (Grand Rapids: Christian University Press, 1987) and the volumes in the Studies in a Christian World View series, edited by Carl F. H. Henry (Grand Rapids: William B. Eerdmans). Titles so far available are *Contours of a World View* by Arthur F. Holmes; *Christianity and Philosophy* by Keith E. Yandell; and *The Person in Psychology* by Mary Stewart Van Leeuwen. Seven other volumes in this series are in preparation. See James W. Sire, *Discipleship of the Mind* (Downers Grove, IL: InterVarsity, 1990) for an extensive bibliography of literature on faith-learning integration, which is an update of an earlier bibliography compiled by Brian J. Walsh and J. Richard Middletown in *The Transforming Vision* (Downers Grove, IL: InterVarsity, 1984).

On Praxis and Christian Higher Education

The address by Nicholas Wolterstorff entitled "The Mission of the Christian College at the End of the 20th Century" has been widely discussed, and is available in an edited version in the June, 1983 issue of *The Reformed Journal* (pp. 14-18). The reader is urged to digest that article as well as Wolterstorff's now classic *Reason Within the Bounds of Religion*, second edition (Grand Rapids: William B. Eerdmans, 1984).

On College and Church

Since both the Christian college and Christian church are communities of believers, they share certain goals such as the acquisition of biblical understanding, the nurturing of spiritual maturity, mutual caring and support, shared worship and sensitizing believers to the needs and problems of the world. Nevertheless, there are at least two kinds of differences: (1) The college extends the concerns of the church by deepening biblical understanding and complementing it with understanding from the academic disciplines to form a coherent world and life view; the college also equips students to address the world's needs and problems that the church has sensitized them to. (2) There is also a real division of labor. For example, the church has as a focus the propagation and preservation of the faith, while the college has as an important focus the initiation of Christians into the academic disciplines with the attendant emphasis on critical dialogue with a larger scholarly community. Also, whereas the church emphasizes religious experience and worship, for the college careful reflection on the meaning and implications of such experience is central. Other divisions of labor could be discussed, but in the long run both the Christian church and Christian college seek the transformation of persons and the larger society. Their distinctives arise from having complementary means to this common end.

CHAPTER 2

POSSIBILITIES AND PRIORITIES:
A DIALOGUE IN WHICH A SKEPTIC CALLS
CHRISTIAN HIGHER EDUCATION TO TASK

Being basically skeptical of this whole enterprise called "Christian higher education," I decided to have it out once and for all with a couple of my acquaintances, both of whom have been associated for many years with academically respected Christian colleges. I invited both of these scholars to my home for an evening's chat around the fireplace. Dean Zufrieden was an able defender of the traditional Christian liberal arts college, while my friend Professor Verbessern was known as a loyal critic of Christian liberal arts education as it now exists.

After my guests had arrived we gathered around the living room in the most comfortable chairs in the house, each eagerly awaiting an evening of intellectually stimulating disagreement. Both guests declined my offer of wine, but Verbessern asked for permission to light his pipe. We began.

"Gentlemen," I said, going straight to the point, "I think you have wasted half of your lives on a second-rate enterprise."

Zufrieden looked up sharply, while Verbessern continued to tamp the tobacco into the bowl of his pipe, waiting for what I was going to say next. "Explain yourself, man," demanded Zufrieden.

"Well," I continued, "both of you are first rate scholars who could be teaching in any of the best universities in the country. Yet you have chosen to teach exclusively Christian students in a hot-house atmosphere that effectively protects them (to their detriment, I fear) from exposure to other than Christian points of view. Furthermore. . . ."

"Now wait just a moment," interrupted Zufrieden. "That assertion is based on a number of assumptions that I simply do not accept."

"I was about to say," I persisted, "that you could have been of much greater service to the Kingdom of God teaching in a secular university, influencing students and colleagues there, and allowing really capable Christian young people to cut their intellectual teeth on the real meat of academic work. I am of the opinion, gentlemen, that Christian colleges are for second rate teachers to spoon feed second rate students. You are both too good for that."

There was a protracted, rather uncomfortable silence. The fire in the fireplace snapped several times. I was beginning to think I had been too blunt, when Verbessern finally completed the lighting of his pipe, took it out of his mouth and cleared his throat. "The existence of counterfeit money does not prove that genuine bills are of no value," he said. "Suppose we admit at the beginning that there are second rate institutions of higher learning that call themselves 'Christian.' That fact no more disqualifies excellent Christian higher education than poor education at a public university proves that all public university education is below par."

"I don't agree with that analogy. . . ," I began.

"No! No! It is quite to the point! There may be good or bad education at either Christian or secular institutions," inserted Zufrieden.

I was a little irritated that they had missed my point. "Look! I was not saying that in practice Christian education happens to be poor, sometimes or often. What I was getting at is that there really isn't any such a thing as **Christian** higher education, good or bad. We have been misplacing our resources in funding Christian colleges. The only advantage of these schools, if there is any, is the fact that education takes place in a religious atmosphere — chapel, prayer meetings, Christian fellowship — that sort of thing. These are things that a Christian at a secular university can get by attending church, having Christian friends and joining a Christian collegiate fellowship and study group. I've already made it clear that I don't value the purely protective aspects of a Christian campus."

"I, for one, am glad that you have stated your position so clearly," responded Zufrieden. "Now we can assess the adequacy of your analysis."

"It appears to me that your account of a Christian college is founded on two misleading ideas. The first is that what makes a Christian college 'Christian' is principally its atmosphere—chapel, fellowship, opportunities for service, and so on. The second misleading idea is that scholarship and instruction are religiously neutral, as if the content of, say a psychology or literature course, would be the same anywhere — just well or poorly taught. I think that both of these ideas are demonstrably false."

"Demonstrably?" I questioned, feeling a little uncomfortable at the precision of his restatement of my position and buying a little time.

"Of course you know what I mean." Zufrieden was a bit impatient with me. "Not 'demonstrably' in the mathematical sense, but in the same rough and ready way we use the term in ordinary language."

"Of course," I withdrew my red herring.

Zufrieden continued relentlessly. "The first of your misleading ideas depends on the second. Christian higher education must consist merely of add-on's if and only if education is a philosophically and religiously neutral activity. Now really, I can't believe that even you are naive enough to believe that."

I decided to wait before responding.

"Now suppose you tell me if you think that all psychology courses at the secular universities across the country are the same." He wasn't about to let me escape.

"No," I admitted.

"Why?"

"Because some psychologists will teach from the perspective of a behaviorist, some from a cognitive perspective, some from a phenomenological perspective, and so forth. They will all cover a lot of the same material, though," I added hastily.

"But the pervasive orientation toward the material will not be neutral, will it?" He pressed.

"I suppose not."

"Would the same thing be true in literature?" Zufrieden asked.

"I would have thought you would have used biology and the issue of evolution as your example," I said with sneer in my voice. The ruse didn't get me off the hook.

"Literature!" he repeated. "Would the same be true in literature?"

"The same texts would be read," I tried to avoid his point once more.

"But the ways in which the texts were approached and the critical theories behind the teachers' approaches would differ." It wasn't clear if this was a question or an assertion.

"That's true," I agreed with some reluctance. I thought I began to see where this was headed.

"Well," he now continued with a hint of triumph in his voice, "every teacher approaches his or her discipline with convictions, either tacit or explicit, about the nature, significance, and proper approach to its subject matter. The great twentieth century philosopher, Alfred North Whitehead, once admitted that every term, regardless of the topics, he always taught the same courses: Whitehead I, Whitehead II and Whitehead III. While it may not be quite so obvious in some disciplines it is still always the case that all teachers who are not simply hacks have visions of the inner workings of their disciplines that stem from their own philosophical and religious perspectives.

"Since this is so, why not permit Christian scholars to gather into an educational community where they can initiate learners into the disciplines from explicit and worked-out Christian perspectives? Why should every student have to reinvent the wheel, when he or she could benefit from the thinking of experienced Christian academicians?

"Far from wasting our lives, Verbessern here and I are investing them in the next generations of young scholars who are going to advance Christian thinking about the intellectual and moral issues that face our society and the church.

"Now you see that the second of your misleading ideas is false, partly by your own admission. The academic enterprise is not religiously and philosophically neutral. And since the truth of your first idea, that Christian higher education is essentially a bunch of add-on worship services in a certain emotional environment, depends on that second idea, it too is false. A Christian college is not a regular college program with Christian embellishments; it is a community of Christian scholars initiating learners into doing their disciplines in a Christian way, and corporately working together to refine and apply a Christian view of life and the world."

I was stunned by this articulate and persuasive vision of the Christian college. Somehow my charges about second rate teachers and protection of students seemed pretty pale as I sat trying to defend my ideas against these two highly capable thinkers. I began to grope for some means of saving face, at least a bit.

"Tell me some more about what this ideal Christian college professor does," I said. I was searching for a comeback.

Zufrieden couldn't resist the bait. "In the first place, Christian college teachers must be respectable scholars in their own right. This means their attitude toward their own disciplines will not be defensive, but they will see their disciplines as legitimate areas of Christian activity and exploration. They will be intent on extending Christian understanding, not just defending the faith. In part this means that Christian college teachers will be operating out of a unified Christian vision of the world, both natural and human. We often call this a Christian world view. Such a unified vision must, for the Christian, be held together by biblical and theological ideas and themes. That makes it distinctively Christian.

"In any case, the primary function of Christian professors is to be mentors to students who are 'apprentices' in their disciplines. The role of the undergraduate teacher is to initiate the student into doing sociology, or philosophy or physics or whatever. And doing it, of course, within a Christian perspective. I might add too, that a Christian teacher ought to be a good model of how a Christian applies Christian understanding to action in the world. Christian teachers should show how the development of intellectual expertise, which is the primary concern of the college, relates to the concerns of a real, caring, serving human being."

Zufrieden stopped short, apparently wanting to say more, but realizing that he had begun to lecture rather than simply converse. Slowly a lens dropped into place for me. I saw the Achilles heel of Zufrieden's vision. I might not win this argument, but he was not going to get away unscathed. I didn't even think he saw the opening he had given me. I smiled a little inwardly.

"All right," I said. "Now let me ask you a few questions." He nodded. Verbessern tapped his pipe to empty it. He had been following intently without getting involved. I sensed he was going to hear me out now before breaking his silence. I began my counterattack mildly.

"Your ideal teacher sounds like quite a person. He or she must be a competent scholar in a specialized field, but must also be at least minimally proficient in theology and philosophy as well."

"Absolutely!" responded Zufrieden, apparently pleased that I had caught on so quickly.

"It sounds to me," I continued, "that this person will have thought deeply about the assumptions that inform the discipline she is teaching and subjected them to philosophical and theological scrutiny. Then she will have rethought the discipline, approaching it from a positive Christian perspective. I guess she will also need the expertise to relate it to an overall theological framework and a philosophically articulate world view. Right?"

"Exactly!" replied Zufrieden, beaming. Verbessern, however, was frowning. I wondered if he saw the trap I was laying.

I tripped the spring. "How many teachers at your college even come close to approximating your ideal?"

Zufrieden opened his mouth as if to speak, but reconsidered. He appeared to be thinking fast. I heard Verbessern give a short, snorting laugh.

"He's got you there, Zufrieden," he joined in at last. "You know as well as I do that there are at most a handful of faculty at most Christian colleges who come anywhere near matching that description. Most Christian college professors are dedicated and capable teachers, with good intentions about relating their faith to their disciplines, but a lot of them are theological novices and philosophically illiterate, not to say allergic to philosophy."

"Hey, wait. . . ." began Zufrieden.

"Zufrieden, let's talk specifics," I said in a loud voice. Everything stopped. "OK, suppose I were to ask you what kind of education it takes to make someone biblically and theologically competent to be your ideal teacher. Would regular church attendance do it?"

"Regrettably, not," Zufrieden replied.

"Would the several undergraduate courses required of students by your college do it?"

"Possibly for a few, especially bright students who did a lot of reading and discussing on their own, but unfortunately it would not be adequate for most."

"Have most of your own faculty had even that much formal theological training?"

He thought a moment. "I suppose not."

"What is the situation with respect to philosophical expertise?"

"Almost certainly much worse," Zufrieden admitted, "but I'm not sure that. . . ."

"Precisely the point I wanted to make." I ignored his last words. "Your claims are impressive, but you can't produce the goods. How could you possibly do for your students what you claim to do, when your teachers cannot do it for themselves?

"Are your teachers, especially those educated exclusively at secular schools, given any special preparation to participate in this admittedly exacting enterprise you have so capably described, or should I say dreamed out loud?"

Zufrieden was clearly feeling defensive now. At least I had evened the score a bit.

"We send our new faculty to a two-week workshop on integrating faith and learning."

"Two weeks! But you just told me that several semester courses were not adequate."

"Well, it is an introduction. It orients their concern. It is a process, after all. And they have the possibility of continuing dialogue with other faculty, including philosophy and biblical and theological studies faculty."

Verbessern had heard enough. "Zufrieden, these are all bandaids on a big wound. They don't come anywhere near meeting the need and you know it well. You have devoted whole summers to giving workshops like that and you know how little can be accomplished in them. You know how little time faculty have for real dialogue in the midst of teaching. You know only too well that at many Christian colleges the Bible department faculty are too concerned with narrowly exegetical concerns to risk getting tangled up in these broad theological, not to mention philosophical, issues. Frankly, I don't think we do nearly so well by our students as you suggested. Even our requirements and special integrative courses seem to me to be too little or too late, or both, even assuming that we had faculty who were prepared to do what you described."

I was about to say something but clearly this had become an internal debate between two advocates of Christian higher education. I decided that listening was a safer course.

Zufrieden had partly risen out of his chair, but Verbessern pressed on, his pipe forgotten. "You speak of initiating students into the task of the Christian scholar. Let's set aside, for the moment, the ability of your teachers to gain adequate background to do this. Let's assume that they are all outstanding Christian scholars of the sort we need. I submit that even then the present format of a traditional liberal arts curriculum and usual size college classes would make your ideal of education unrealizable.

"Let's just take class size, for example. How large are your classes?"

Zufrieden considered a moment, then said "Generally thirty-five to fifty in lower level courses and fifteen to thirty in upper level courses."

"Do you really think that you can function as a mentor who initiates students into your vision of the discipline in a class of forty or fifty?"

"Well, not really at that level, but the situation improves with advanced classes. Besides, all students have access to me outside of class for individual dialogue."

"But," responded Verbessern, "**most** of the students in the whole college are only exposed to you in those large classes. It's only a few who go on to take advanced courses. Furthermore, I would be willing to bet that the number of students who avail themselves of your time outside of class is minuscule compared to the size of the student body."

"Right on both counts," admitted Zufrieden, "But I still maintain that what we do, with all of our constraints, is qualitatively different from education at a secular college. I maintain that even if I grant all of the criticisms you both have advanced, the Christian college is still **educationally** distinctive. We do achieve our goals, though in an admittedly limited way."

"Something is better than nothing," I supplied.

"Exactly!" said Zufrieden.

"Well," Verbessern seemed about to lay his cards on the table, "I think I see a problem with the way the Christian liberal arts college has evolved.

Our argument here tonight reveals both the strengths and the weaknesses of our sort of institution. At least in the United States we have tried to unite a traditional liberal arts curriculum with faith-learning integration and your concept of initiating students through a mentor. We have almost canonized the concept of the 'Christian liberal arts college.' We even hang onto this terminology when we have added large vocational components, and claim that 'liberal arts' is an attitude rather than a curricular structure, history to the contrary.

"Here's the problem: commitment to a traditional liberal arts curricular structure strains our resources and places requirements on our students that leave both students and institution less time and resources to pursue those **distinctives** of Christian higher education. It is a sad fact that when the educational (and economic) chips are down we almost always favor academic and vocational disciplines over interdisciplinary and theological integration. Our students often get a first rate college education, but only a second (or third) rate initiation into exploring the philosophical and theological significance of their academic disciplines and their place in a Christian view of life and the world."

"But at least we do **try** to do that," responded Zufrieden. "Furthermore, you cannot judge how much we do to integrate faith and learning just by looking at the courses that a student takes. There is a great deal more that goes on in college than courses taken in classrooms. Students are encouraged to carry their academic studies into their practical lives and social activities. There are opportunities for service in the real world that require insights from both the student's academic expertise and her faith perspective. Why, even in student development . . ."

"Funny you should bring that up," interrupted Verbessern, "because that is exactly a matter that was going through my mind. As a point of fact I think you have touched upon a genuine strength of the best of the Christian colleges." Zufrieden visibly relaxed at these words from Verbessern and settled back into his chair with the look of a parent who is hearing his child praised. This lasted only momentarily, however, as Verbessern continued.

"Yet even here at a point of strength the deficiencies show. All of the co-curricular programs and activities you allude to exist essentially as a side-by-side add-on to the regular program. The fault lies on both sides. The student development people are so careful to defend the importance of the social, emotional and service aspects of the student's lives that they resist the intrusion of cognitive, critical and intellectually oriented emphases into their bailiwick. On the other side, the faculty, even those in academic disciplines which have much to offer the students in orienting their reflection on action and life experiences, are only interested in preserving the academic purity of their disciplines. They have very little interest in exploring ways in which their disciplines may be responsive to the needs of the world. They are certainly not aggressive in engaging students in critical Christian reflection on practical applications of the disciplines. They rarely see themselves as exemplars of responsibly engaged academicians.

"We really need to take seriously our rhetoric that neither students nor faculty can be split into discrete, isolated parts, but are whole, integrated unities. Christianity clearly implies that such holistic, integrated human beings must bring all that they are, including their intellects, to all of their actions. I truly fear that we have failed to do this effectively in Christian higher education, in spite of a few notable successes."

I knew that this speech had hit Zufrieden hard, because I had often heard him complain of the weak way in which co-curricular activities supported the integrative activities of the academic program. Verbessern, however, seemed to have gone even further in advocating that the academic program in turn support the student development program. In fact the distinction between curricular and co-curricular seemed to be itself in question according to Verbessern's view.

"But at least we do **try**," repeated Zufrieden with a slight hint of a whine in his voice.

"So we do," continued Verbessern. "But it's a question of priorities. What if our priority were to make sure our students were given all the personal equipment necessary to be first rate praxis-oriented Christian scholars by having fine Christian mentors working with them on an intimate basis, individualizing their programs of studies over however long it took, disregarding all the constraints we have imposed on ourselves by being part of mainstream American liberal arts colleges. The issue is clearly a question of priorities. Do we **really** believe in our own distinctives?"

"It would never be able to pay for itself," I commented, thinking myself wise beyond all question.

"Of course not," said Verbessern. "Neither do babies, flower gardens, or medical missionaries."

We sat for a while in thoughtful silence.

"I say," observed Zufrieden, "I do believe the fire has gone out."

CHAPTER 3

BANDAIDS AND ORGAN TRANSPLANTS:
SOME CURRENT EFFORTS AT INNOVATION

We are not the first to perceive that the established structure of the traditional liberal arts college is not an altogether satisfactory vehicle for accomplishing the distinctive ends of Christian higher education. There are a number of innovative approaches to accomplishing those ends already in existence. Some of these amount to little more than bandaids on the body of an existing college, while others go so far as to transplant an entirely new structure on an existing institution. In this chapter we briefly will examine representative examples of these innovations. Our discussion focuses on each of these as attempts to achieve the distinctives outlined in Chapter 1. The reader must not judge other aspects of the programs solely on the basis of our treatment here.

The programs discussed below are very diverse. Some of them are aimed at undergraduate students. Others approach the task of fulfilling the distinctive goals of Christian higher education on the graduate level. Still other of these programs address the problem of preparing faculty to accomplish these goals in existing settings. As might be expected from such diversity, the programs are highly variable in how radically they revise the existing priorities in the direction of the priorities to which the catalogs give lip service. The programs vary considerably in the depth to which they address these goals. This, of course, is due in part to their various assumptions concerning the prior preparation of the students or faculty involved in the programs.

ALTERNATIVE APPROACHES TO CHRISTIAN HIGHER EDUCATION AT THE UNDERGRADUATE LEVEL

Short-term Undergraduate Programs

A number of Christian colleges provide short-term programs designed with the distinctive goals of Christian higher education in mind. Such programs may provide a summer or one-semester opportunity for work and study through an internship in the student's intended career field. This is usually combined with appropriate seminars dealing with issues relevant to the practice of that career. Such seminars often emphasize a multi-disciplinary approach to the issues pertinent to the given career, and there is generally a deliberate attempt to apply distinct Christian perspectives to these issues. An example of this approach is the American Studies Program sponsored by the Christian College Coalition in Washington, D.C.,[7] which provides a one-semester opportunity for work and study through an internship in a professional setting within the student's major field of study. Students earn eight credits, combined with four two-credit study modules on Foundations for Public Involvement, Domestic Policy Issues, Economic Policy Issues and International Policy Issues.

These short-term undergraduate programs generally involve a limited number of students, with emphasis placed on small group interaction and close relationships between faculty mentors and students. One such semester program (The Oregon Extension) emphasizes community living, with shared participation in food preparation, maintenance chores, recreation, travel, and worship experiences. This is integrated with rigorous interdisciplinary study segments on Contemporary Society, Social Analysis and Theory, The Human Condition and the Christian Faith. This integration emphasizes the relationship of learning to everyday life.

It is clear that such short-term undergraduate programs can be designed to place primary emphasis on the goals of exploring knowledge across disciplines, developing an integrated Christian conceptual frame-

---

[7]Other examples of short-term programs may be found in the Notes on Chapter 3, along with addresses for all of the programs mentioned.

work, and promoting academic initiation through close mentor/student relationships. Depending on the nature of the internships and concurrent seminars, they may also be effective vehicles for developing a sense of responsibility and acquiring knowledge for addressing problems facing the world
(e.g., public policy issues or environmental concerns). There are also signs
of emphasis on non-cognitive development intended to complement cognitive development, through appropriate worship and other forms of community activities. But though these emphases are indeed primary during the
short-term programs, the troublesome question is whether they are a secondary aspect of a student's program from the perspective of her four-year
undergraduate experience. For all their outstanding educational value, they
appear to be add-on's or interludes from "academic business as usual."
They are excellent instances of initiation relative to the distinctive goals of
Christian higher education, but where does one go after initiation?
Furthermore, the complexity of issues that demand multi-disciplinary
scholarship suggest the need for a more substantial undertaking than short-
term initiation.

Undergraduate Models Deemphasizing Career Preparation

There are a few residential undergraduate colleges in the Catholic tradition that intend to be "purist" relative to the liberal arts tradition, without
the encumbrances of career or job preparation (apparently relegated to
post-graduate study). These institutions place heavy emphasis on a common core of knowledge required of all students. Such requirements typically include foundational studies in the areas of philosophy, literature, history, and theology, with a "great books" approach sometimes being used. In
addition, there generally are required studies in mathematics and the natural sciences, as well as in foreign languages.

In one such model, at Thomas Aquinas College, students follow a
common prescribed four-year course of study in small group settings, consisting of a four-year theology tutorial (a study of the Bible and the Fathers
of the Church), a three-year philosophy tutorial (decidedly Thomistic in
emphasis), a four-year mathematics tutorial (including "pure mathematics"
and astronomy), a two-year language tutorial in Latin, a one-year logic
tutorial, a one-year music tutorial, a four-year Laboratory (devoted to the

investigation of nature through experiment), and a four-year Seminar (devoted to reading the greatest works in literature and history). There is no requirement for specialized study in an academic discipline. In another version of this approach at the Thomas More College of Liberal Arts, students may pursue a major in literature, philosophy, or political science.

Since institutions of this type are not bound to a curriculum organized around academic majors dictated by career concerns, they may exercise various other options for curricular organization. One possibility is the organization of knowledge around the traditional divisional categories: the humanities, the natural sciences, the social sciences, and the fine arts. It remains an open question at this point as to which principles for organizing knowledge would be most conducive to accomplishing the primary distinctives of Christian higher education in a setting where career preparation is de-emphasized.

This "purist" approach to Christian higher education is particularly conducive to emphasizing the exploration of knowledge across disciplines and the development of an integrated Christian conceptual framework. Such emphases will not be add-on's or interludes from overt career preparation. Rather, they will be the primary emphasis of four years of cognitive development. However, there may be a tendency in those developing such models to place only secondary or derivative emphasis on the goals of non-cognitive development and the development of a sense of responsibility for overtly addressing the needs and problems facing the church and world. An adequate model for Christian higher education must also incorporate these emphases, as well as a suitable role for career preparation, properly understood (more about this later).

Satellite Christian Colleges

A few Christian colleges have situated themselves as satellite colleges affiliated with secular universities. Messiah College (PA) has a Philadelphia campus adjacent to Temple University. A residential Living-Learning Center offers the educational advantages of a large university and the cultural advantages of a major city. Junior or senior students may elect an enrichment semester at the Philadelphia campus, taking one course at the

Center from a Messiah faculty member, with the remainder of their courses taken at Temple. In addition, several academic majors have been designed in collaboration with Temple, with students typically taking their first two years at Messiah's main campus and their last two years at the Philadelphia campus, completing their requirements at Temple, but with degrees awarded by Messiah College.

Conrad Grebel College of the University of Waterloo (Ontario, Canada) exemplifies a more integral relationship with a public university. Conrad Grebel is one of four Christian church colleges located at, and affiliated (or federated) with, the University of Waterloo. Founded by the Mennonites of Ontario, Conrad Grebel may offer instruction in any course in the arts, humanities, or social sciences, subject to approval of the University Senate. All degree students in such courses are registered with the university, and the Conrad Grebel faculty hold university appointments. Since all Conrad Grebel students are registered with the university, they will generally take many of their courses in various university departments or at one or more of the other church colleges. Some students may take only one Conrad Grebel course, while others take full minors or majors at the college. The college presently teaches courses in Interdisciplinary Arts, History, Music, Peace and Conflict Studies, Philosophy, Religious Studies and Sociology. The integral relationship between Christian college and public university exemplified by Conrad Grebel College fits well with the Canadian system of higher education, which does not provide for the existence of independent private colleges, but, rather, requires all degree-granting colleges to be affiliated in some fashion with public universities.

There is at least one example in the United States that is similar to the Conrad Grebel example, but at the graduate level. The Psychological Studies Institute in Atlanta, Georgia was founded to promote training, research, counseling and service in the field of mental health from an interdenominational, evangelical perspective, with emphasis on promoting an understanding of the relationship between psychology and theology. A graduate program is offered through a cooperative arrangement with the Department of Counseling and Psychological Services at Georgia State University. Students at the Institute complete degree requirements at Georgia State University toward a Master of Science degree in Community Counseling. University courses are taught by full-time faculty of Georgia State University and faculty within the Institute who hold adjunct appointments with the university. The Institute complements the university courses in the M.S. program with additional studies in counseling, psychology, biblical interpretation, theology, and integration of psychology and theology, as well as through a counseling practicum at a counseling center operated by the Institute. This complementary study and practicum experience leads to a Diploma in Christian Counseling from the Institute in addition to the M.S. awarded by the University.

Satellite Christian colleges affiliated with secular universities can be particularly effective in accomplishing the goals of non-cognitive development, and the promotion of academic initiation through close mentor/student relationships on the satellite campus. If properly designed the combined college/university program of study can also be an effective vehicle for developing a sense of responsibility and acquiring knowledge for addressing problems facing the world, as well as for acquiring broad understanding in the academic disciplines and biblical and theological study, and the development of an integrated Christian conceptual framework. However, certain nagging questions persist as to the achievable depth of accomplishment of these latter two goals using this model. In particular, if the student's undergraduate education is under the dual auspices of separate Christian and secular institutions, can sufficient emphasis be placed on truly integrating knowledge claims flowing from different presuppositions or will there rather be a tendency to settle for co-existence, at best, between two sets of knowledge claims? Or, will the study at the satellite campus degenerate into supplying "correctives" to university learning that may be based on presuppositions antithetical to the Christian faith? It appears to us that this model will be most effective if steps are taken to orchestrate faculty and student dialogue between members of the satellite Christian college and other members of the university. Assuming that some common ground exists, this will maximize the potential that persons holding to different sets of presuppositions will learn from one another.

The constructive model that we propose in chapter 4 bears some similiarities to the satellite campus model. It calls for foundational Christian studies, engagement with public universities and synthesis of these two sources of knowledge. However, it does not try to do all of this at the undergraduate level, which at best results only in preliminary initiation into such demanding activities, or in a self-contained graduate program. Rather, our model will emphasize foundational Christian study during the under-graduate years, engagement with public universities at the graduate level, to be followed by in-depth synthesis at the post-graduate school level.

ALTERNATIVE APPROACHES TO CHRISTIAN EDUCATION AT THE GRADUATE LEVEL

Master's Programs for the Laity

A number of models presently exist that provide the opportunity for laypersons to obtain masters degrees in Christian studies. This approach allows for either part-time or summer study, as well as a more concentrated one-year program of full-time study. The emphasis in such programs is on developing a strong biblical, theological, historical, and ethical foundation for the life and work of a Christian layperson in the world. For example, New College for Advanced Christian Studies, Berkeley, offers a one-year Master of Christian Studies program with requirements including courses such as Ministry of the Laity, Old Testament and New Testament, Christian Theology, Evangelical Ethics or Biblical Ethics, an integrative studies project, and electives in biblical, theological, historical, ethical, or other studies. A more intensive Master of Arts program allows students to major in one of the following five areas: Biblical Studies, Theology, Christian Ethics, Cross-Cultural Studies, and Christian Studies (interdisciplinary/integrative areas).

It is apparent that programs of this nature have been designed, in varying degrees, to help Christian laypersons realize the goals of exploring knowledge across disciplines, developing an integrated Christian conceptual framework, and developing the expertise for addressing the needs and problems facing the church and world (by means of their chosen careers). Furthermore, the relatively small size of programs of this nature makes it possible to emphasize close contact between faculty and students and allows for individual attention to student development, thus fostering individual educational relationships between mentors and students.

These models are indeed commendable ministries to the educational needs of many Christian laypersons, but some difficult questions must be faced. First, one observes that the requirements for some of these masters programs do not evidence breadth or depth of study beyond the typical B.A. core curriculum requirements in most Christian liberal arts colleges. If the target audience of laypersons is composed primarily of those who attended secular colleges or universities, such requirements are appropriate. Yet this suggests that this graduate level program does not advance students beyond what is arguably inadequate even as undergraduate Christian education in the light of our educational distinctives. It would not add much of significance to those who already had such undergraduate courses, especially if the classes had a mix of those who did and did not attend Christian colleges.

Furthermore, what is available at the master's level for those who by some means have secured adequate foundational Christian studies as undergraduates? It would seem that greater depth of study is needed for certain sectors of the Christian laity, such as those preparing for vocations as Christian scholars in academic settings, or those involved in the political arena where the struggle with complex public policy issues requires deeper levels of cross-disciplinary and integrative understanding.

Master's Programs Built on Undergraduate Foundational Studies

Whereas master's degree programs designed primarily for the laity do not generally presuppose any specific type of undergraduate preparation, an alternative approach is to design master's degree programs that presuppose specific types of undergraduate preparation. A number of these programs have emerged at Christian colleges in recent years, with curricular specializations generally in professional areas such as education, nursing or business administration. One unique program in this category is the Master of Business Administration or Master of Science Program in Economic Development for the global or urban poor offered by Eastern College. This program is based on the "scriptural imperative to serve the poor," and is designed to "train a new kind of missionary who has a capability for helping the socially disinherited to participate in economically productive business enterprises." This program consciously places primary emphasis on developing a sense of responsibility and providing the knowledge and skills necessary for addressing problems facing major sectors of the world.

It is significant to note that there is not a flurry of activity at Christian colleges to establish master's degree programs in the arts and sciences that would enable a student to spend a year or two in concentrated study of the relationship between the Christian faith and the academic discipline in which she majored as an undergraduate. One leading Christian college did have a Master of Arts Program in Christian Studies that provided for such integrative study within major divisions of knowledge such as the fine arts, the humanities, the social sciences or the natural sciences. But this strong program had to be discontinued due primarily to lack of enrollment. One can only speculate as to the reasons. Possibly such programs are viewed as not having adequate "vocational payoff" in terms of job preparation. Possibly recent college graduates do not typically share the passion for developing a carefully articulated coherent Chrsitian framework. Possibly those who are interested in such advanced integrative study prefer available doctoral programs (as described in the next section). At any rate, we believe this is an important sub-group of potential master's degree programs since these programs would truly presuppose and build upon foundational studies at the undergraduate level, placing primary emphasis at a deep level on the related goals of exploring knowledge across disciplines and developing an integrated Christian conceptual framework.

Doctoral Programs in Selected Academic Disciplines

The reader should note the apparent increase in depth of study as we proceed from the category of master's programs in Christian higher education designed primarily for the Christian laity to masters programs that strictly build upon some undergraduate foundational study in Christian thought and specialized academic disciplines. The next logical step in this progression in depth of study is the development of doctoral programs in selected academic disciplines that emphasize the development of Christian perspectives on these disciplines. A few models of this nature are presently in existence.

One model of this approach is the doctoral program in clinical psychology at Biola University's Rosemead School of Psychology, designed primarily to train practitioners in clinical psychology. Although research training is not the main emphasis in this program, it does include those aspects of human research that are of relevance to clinical psychologists. The primary goal of this doctoral program is the in-depth relating of the data and concepts of psychology to those of Christian theology. This goal is based on the belief that since both psychology and theology address the human condition there is a great deal to be gained by interdisciplinary study of human nature. The program presupposes strong undergraduate preparation in psychology. This model is an exemplary instance of primary commitment to the goals of exploring knowledge across disciplines and developing an integrated Christian conceptual framework, with significant emphasis on preparing Christians to address the needs and problems facing the church and world.

A second existing model of this approach is a doctoral program in philosophy at the Institute for Christian Studies in Toronto, intended for persons whose vocational goal is a life of scholarship and teaching in or related to philosophy or the philosophy of a particular field of study. This model emphasizes the interrelationships between biblical study, theology and philosophy and seeks to help students in almost any field of study to understand their field in a Christian way. The method for developing such understanding is to concentrate on the fundamental points in a given discipline where theological, philosophical and methodological questions arise. This model emphasizes individual educational relationships between mentors and students by its organization as an academic community of senior members and junior members at work in research and learning, even sharing responsibility for governance of the program. A special merit of this model is its crucial and valid recognition that the foundation for all Christian study lies not only in the areas of biblical study and theology, but also in philosophy, wherein Christians must come to grips with the most fundamental epistemological questions concerning ways of knowing and justification of belief systems, ontological questions concerning the ultimate nature of reality, and axiological questions concerning values and moral obligations. This is another exemplary instance of primary in-depth commitment to the goals of exploring knowledge across disciplines and developing an integrated Christian conceptual framework.

A comparison of present approaches to Christian higher education with the graduate programs discussed above reveals great variations in the depth of interdisciplinary and integrative study available in existing models for Christian higher education. Eventually, we must deal with the issue of which depth of study is most appropriate for each Christian person. We will address this in our constructive proposal in the next chapter. We will also explore the problem that whereas existing models for doctoral programs provide in-depth interdisciplinary and integrative preparation for careers in selected fields (practitioners in clinical psychology or academic careers in philosophy), such in-depth preparation is not presently available in other important fields through which Christians need to influence the academic community, the church and the world. More importantly, there are no programs in which a student can immerse herself in interdisciplinary and integrative studies at the undergraduate level.

ALTERNATIVE APPROACHES TO FACULTY DEVELOPMENT AND SCHOLARSHIP

As noted in the previous chapter, faculty members at a typical undergraduate Christian college often face two related problems. First, their graduate degrees are generally earned in highly specialized academic fields, thus leaving them ill-prepared for interdisciplinary and integrative teaching or scholarship. They generally have a lot of self-study (catching-up) to do. A related problem is that the heavy combination of teaching, student advising and institutional service demands typically placed on such faculty members leaves minimal time or energy to prepare for and pursue the enormous new task of interdisciplinary and integrative teaching or scholarship. It is obvious to us that models must be available to make these tasks possible, and that in these models the interdisciplinary and integrative tasks must be primary rather than secondary responsibilities.

Short-term Programs for Faculty Development and Scholarship

One existing approach toward faculty development and scholarship of an interdisciplinary and integrative nature consists of short-term programs for Christian college faculty members. An example is the annual "Christianity and the Liberal Arts" summer workshop for new faculty at Christian colleges sponsored by the Christian College Coalition. The initial portion of such programs typically consist of guest lecturer presentations on general integrative topics, with emphasis placed on biblical, theological, philosophical and historical foundations. The faculty participants then begin preliminary work on the implications of these general integrative themes for their teaching and/or scholarship in their respective academic disciplines, under the tutelage of the guest lecturers.

These short-term programs are excellent vehicles for acquainting faculty with interdisciplinary and integrative teaching or scholarship. However since their duration may range from a few days to at most two weeks, they can hardly be viewed as a primary emphasis within the year-long responsibilities of a typical faculty participant. They are exciting interludes, enough to whet the appetite, but more primary models are needed.

Institutes for Advanced Christian Learning and Scholarship

An initial step toward a more primary model for faculty development and scholarship of an interdisciplinary and integrative nature was taken with the establishment of the Institute for Advanced Christian Studies (IFACS). This institute sponsors interdisciplinary and integrative workshops and research by selected Christian scholars and has resulted in the publication of a number of excellent books (e.g., the current series on *Studies in a Christian World View*, published by William B. Eerdmans). However, the original intention of providing a location where Christian scholars can come together for intense periods of study has not materialized. Financial support provided by IFACS for serious interdisciplinary and integrative scholarship is surely helpful and a step in the right direction, but much more is needed.

Excellent further steps in the direction of primary models have been taken by various centers for Christian study and scholarship where faculty members can spend a full year working on scholarly projects of an interdisciplinary and integrative nature. For example, at the Calvin Center for Christian Scholarship an important practical or theoretical issue is chosen for in-depth interdisciplinary study during a given academic year. A team of six to eight scholars is assembled, consisting of approximately three faculty members from Calvin College, three visiting faculty members and two or three students from Calvin.

Visiting faculty members are expected to do some teaching during their one-year term of appointment. Issues chosen for study at the Calvin Center have included Christian Stewardship and Natural Resources, Public Justice and Educational Equity, a Reformed View of Faith and Reason, Christian Economic Theory and Activity, The Nature and Role of the Behavioral Sciences, The Theory and Practice of Hermeneutics, The Search for Responsible Technology, and Creation and Cosmogony. The results of each year of intensive study have typically been published in book form. This is a model where for one year faculty members do indeed have primary responsibility for research and scholarship, with a clear emphasis on the goals of integrating knowledge across disciplines and developing a Christian conceptual framework for interpreting and acting in the world. Depending on the nature of the issue dealt with, this type of center can also be an important vehicle for developing the understanding and skills needed to address needs and problems facing the church and the world. Such programs can also be designed to foster individual educational relationships between learners and the formation of a learning community committed to realization of some of the distinctive goals for Christian higher education. Possibly some of these goals could be achieved even more significantly if these types of primary responsibilities could be extended for more than one year.

Associations for Christian Praxis

A number of associations have been formed to encourage Christians to become more actively involved in addressing contemporary social and political problems. The Center for Public Justice builds its agenda on the biblical call for justice for all peoples, independent of religious commitment. The Institute on Religion and Democracy emphasizes the interrelationships between justice, peace and liberty. These organizations have significant educational ministries, including the publication of newsletters, the preparation of position papers and other pamphlets and study materials on current issues, and the conducting of national and regional conferences. At times they have also served an active role in the legislative process by giving testimony before congressional committees.

It is obvious that these associations for Christian praxis are particularly appropriate for accomplishing the goal of developing a sense of responsibility and acquiring knowledge for addressing problems facing the world. Such knowledge reflects a synthesis of biblical knowledge with understanding from the academic disciplines. These associations exemplify an important complement to the Institutes for Advanced Christian Learning and Scholarship discussed in the previous category. Whereas the latter institutes emphasize the important cognitive tasks that are necessary for addressing contemporary issues, the former associations emphasize more active involvement in the political process.

Although they certainly do not neglect the development of cognitive understanding relative to contemporary problems, it could be argued that these praxis-oriented associations would be even more effective if they increased their emphasis on scholarship in areas related to public policy. This could be accomplished by their sponsoring of public policy institutes that would enable Christian scholars to hold long-term appointments working on praxis-oriented scholarship. It is our strong conviction that we must place greater emphasis on creating models that provide Christian scholars with the opportunity to devote primary energy to the interdisciplinary and integrative scholarship so sorely needed if we are adequately to address complex human needs. Of course, the obvious, but difficult task is to create the proper balance between supporting sound scholarship relative to public policy issues and entering the hurly-burly of the political arena in attempts to implement the results of such scholarship.

CONCLUSION

We applaud those who have established the alternative approaches for Christian higher education reviewed in this chapter. They reflect a seriousness about the distinctive goals for such education, although there are obvious gradations in the depth to which these models foster these goals. There are also variations in the extent to which the pursuit of these goals represent secondary or primary responsibilities for participating students and faculty. As the reader has no doubt surmised by now, we have a special appreciation for the existing primary in-depth models, and we have a sense of urgency about the need for the further extension of such models. This brings us to our constructive recommendations.

NOTES ON CHAPTER 3: SAMPLE MODELS

The programs noted below generally exemplify the various approaches to alternative models for Christian higher education that have been described in general terms in the body of this chapter. The details of implementation obviously differ from program to program, even within the same category. Even some of the details noted in the text above change from year to year. Therefore, it is recommended that persons interested in obtaining detailed information about each program listed write directly to the appropriate address indicated below.

Short-Term Undergraduate Programs

American Studies Program/Latin American Studies Program
The Christian College Coalition
327 Eighth St., N.E.
Washington, D.C. 20002-6158

Chicago Metropolitan Center Program
Old Colony Building, Suite 515
407 South Dearborn
Chicago, IL 60605

AuSable Trails Institute of Environmental Studies
Big Twin Lake
Route No. 2
Mancelona, MI 49659

The Oregon Extension Program
15097 Greensprings Highway
Ashland, OR 97520

Undergraduate Models De-emphasizing Vocational Preparation

Thomas Aquinas College
10,000 North Ojai Road
San Paula, CA 93060

The Thomas More College of Liberal Arts
6 Manchester St.
Merrimack, NH 03054

Satellite Christian Colleges

Conrad Grebel College
Waterloo, Ontario N2L 2G6
CANADA

Messiah College
Grantham, PA 17027

The Psychological Studies Institute
2055 Mount Paran Road, N.W.
Atlanta, GA 30327

Master's Programs for the Laity

New College for Advanced Christian Studies,Berkeley
2600 Dwight Way
Berkeley, CA 94704

Regent College
2130 Wesbrook Mall
Vancouver, British Columbia V6T 1W6
CANADA

Institute for Christian Studies
229 College Street
Toronto, Ontario MST 1R4
CANADA

Master's Programs Built on Undergraduate Foundational Studies

MBA Program
Eastern College
Saint Davids, PA 19087

Master of Arts in Communication
Wheaton College
Wheaton, IL 60187

Doctoral Programs in Selected Academic Disciplines

Rosemead School of Psychology
Biola University
13800 Biola Avenue
La Mirada, CA 90639-0001

Institute for Christian Studies
229 College Street
Toronto, Ontario MST 1R4
CANADA

Fuller Theological Seminary
Doctoral Program in Psychology
135 North Oakland
Pasadena, CA 91182

Short-Term Models for Faculty Development and Scholarship

New Faculty Workshop
The Christian College Coalition
327 Eighth St., N.E.
Washington, D.C. 20002-6158

Institutes for Advanced Christian Learning and Scholarship

Institute for Advanced Christian Studies
PO Box 241
Wheaton, IL 60189

Calvin Center for Christian Scholarship
Calvin College
Grand Rapids, MI 49506

Institute for Ecumenical and Cultural Research
St. Johns University
Collegeville, MN 56321

Associations for Christian Praxis

The Center for Public Justice
321 Eighth St., N.E.
Washington, D.C. 20002-6107

The Institute on Religion & Democracy
729 - 15th Street NW
Suite 900
Washington, D.C. 20005

CHAPTER 4

THE SKIN OF OUR TEETH:
THE VERY LEAST WE NEED TO DO

The story is told of an old Vermont farmer, the very epitome of a breed noted for their few words, who made his way to the closest bank a few towns away to cash a check he had received in the mail. Unaccustomed to the ritual of the teller's window, he studied the bank lobby carefully and then queued up in a line to await service. The odors of the barn created a space before and behind him as the teller carefully attended to each customer. Finally the farmer's turn came and the teller told him where to sign, then delivered the money onto the counter in front of him. There followed an enormous lapse of time during which the farmer stood counting and recounting his money, preventing the next customer from getting to the window. In an attempt to find out what was causing the hold-up, the bank's manager made his way to the booth and looked out over the shoulder of the perplexed teller. "Excuse me, sir," said the manager. "Is there some problem?" When he received no immediate reply he tried again. "Pardon me, sir, but did the teller give you the correct amount?" At this the farmer looked up from his counting, remarked laconically, "Just barely," and stalked out.

In most of our institutions we have **not even** "just barely" set our priorities to accomplish the distinctives which we espouse. There is little point in diagnosing the complex sets of conditions and personal decisions that make this so. Directing blame (or accepting it, for that matter) will do little to correct the situation. What is critical is that we begin now to do something about it so that our colleges will not be living according to false priorities, albeit priorities that are often concealed by catalog rhetoric and the good faith efforts of some badly overextended faculty. What follows is an attempt to bring our efforts up to "just barely" accomplishing what we proudly announce that we are all about.

In this chapter we **have not** set ourselves to overturn the existing structure of Christian liberal arts education in some wholesale manner. We **have** attempted to allow ourselves to be guided primarily by the distinctive goals of Christian higher education. What follows are two modest proposals. The first is an agenda of items that should receive priority attention in the context of existing structures. It is a kind of huge bandaid, in the language of the last chapter. The second proposal is like an undergraduate organ transplant in which a new arm is grafted onto the institution as a type of experimental college. This experimental arm could become the seedbed for a whole new breed of Christian scholar, providing teachers for the next generation of Christian higher education.

AN AGENDA FOR EXISTING CHRISTIAN LIBERAL ARTS COLLEGES

If one takes seriously the five distinctive features of Christian higher education, there are significant implications for programming at existing Christian liberal arts colleges. We encourage the governing boards, administration and faculty of such colleges to consider seriously the following concrete proposals, made with the full realization that some of these proposals are already at various stages of implementation at a number of Christian colleges.

First an inevitable financial issue must be faced. It will be apparent that many of the items on the following agenda will require significant institutional funding. This may seem unreasonable in a time when finances are scarce at many Christian colleges. However, it is clearly a matter of priorities. Based on our collective years of teaching at Christian colleges, as well as serving in administrative positions, it is our observation that a college's actual commitment to the distinctives of Christian higher education should not be measured by the college catalog rhetoric, but can be measured more accurately by reading the college's approved budget for any given year. We often allocate significant funding to items that are only peripheral to the distinctives of Christian higher education (e.g., activities primarily designed to keep students from going home on weekends). College governing boards and administrators need to establish new funding priorities that reflect commitment to such distinctives, including substantial funding for the proposals noted below.

Summer Study Programs for Faculty

Establish salaried summer study programs for faculty, either at individual colleges or at regional centers, that will enable faculty to devote full-time energy for at least three months to study that emphasizes the exploration of knowledge across disciplines and the development of an integrated Christian conceptual framework.

Before switching roles from a faculty member to an administrator at a Christian college, one of us engaged another such administrator in conversation. We noted that the difference between the administrator and the faculty member relative to summer expectations was not that one worked while the other didn't. We both worked throughout most of the summer. The only difference was that just one of us was paid. The idea of faculty members having the summer off is antiquated, as is the idea of working for nothing. It is obvious that numerous assignments carried out by faculty members during the regular academic year make it extremely difficult, if not impossible, for such faculty members to engage in significant study exploring knowledge across disciplines and developing an integrated Christian conceptual framework.

Furthermore, many faculty members at Christian colleges come to their initial teaching positions with virtually no educational background relative to these integrative emphases, despite or possibly because of having earned PhD's from prestigious universities. The truth of the matter is that many us were complete novices relative to such integrative themes as we embarked on our teaching careers. The ideal time to remedy that fact is during the extensive summer breaks. Faculty members should be paid for such arduous labors at a rate commensurate with their monthly salary rates during the academic year. Our preference for the design of such self-study programs would be to individualize these programs for faculty members at their own institutions, using the faculty peer mentoring program proposed below.

Summer Research Programs for Faculty

> Establish funded summer research programs for faculty at
> individual colleges that will enable faculty to produce quality
> scholarly work relative to the goals of exploring knowledge
> across disciplines, developing an integrated Christian concep-
> tual framework, and addressing problems facing the church
> and world.

As faculty members progress in their own study relative to integrative
themes, it is important to provide opportunities for them to engage in
research that will lead to quality scholarly publications to be shared with
the larger academic community. Again, the reality of heavy assignments
during the regular academic year suggests the advisability of devoting the
summer months to such research activities. Summer research grants at individual colleges ought to be awarded on a competitive basis, with all
research proposals being evaluated by a suitable panel of scholars, prefer-
ably external to the given institution. Such scholarly activity is not to be
viewed as an add-on to the "real business" of faculty at Christian colleges,
namely teaching, but should be viewed as an indispensable part of what it
means to be a faculty member (teacher/scholar) at such colleges. Funding
for such research activities should include stipends for time worked as well
as provision for covering appropriate research expenses.

Faculty Peer Mentoring Programs

> Senior faculty members should serve as personal mentors to
> junior faculty members in relation to the goals of exploring
> knowledge across disciplines and developing an integrated
> Christian conceptual framework.

The adequate pursuit of these two integrative goals is a lifelong task
for serious faculty members at Christian colleges. The best initiation agent
for a faculty member just beginning this arduous task is a faculty member
who is further along the way. In addition to serving these integrative goals,
this approach will concretely embody the practice of promoting academic
initiation through mentor/apprentice relationships. We personally entered

such a relationship in an informal way during the initial stages of our teaching careers, and can attest to its effectiveness toward fostering these integrative distinctives. Again, due recognition must be given to the magnitude of this mentoring task prior to the time when the apprentice becomes relatively independent of her mentor. The summer months provide ideal times for such mentoring. However, provision should also be made for suitable released time during the academic year for both the mentor and the apprentice to adequately carry out their respective tasks.

Faculty Mentoring of Students Using Individualized Programs of Study

> Establish pilot projects at individual Christian colleges wherein each of four carefully selected faculty members will be assigned to approximately six promising incoming freshmen, with the expected four-year program of study to evolve out of this mentor/apprentice relationship.

It is worth noting again the most fundamental assumption about the nature of education that informs this entire text. We believe that education at its best is very personal, requiring a close mentor/apprentice relationship between teacher and student. We also believe that adequate curricular content can flow from this relationship, even if such content differs from the usual lock-step requirements established at most Christian colleges. We believe it is important to seek such appropriate middle-ground between the much discussed and abused extremes of either "student-centered" education or "teacher- centered" education. Both of these extremes are destructive of the dialogue inherent in effective mentoring.

Recognizing the radical nature of this mentoring approach, we therefore propose the following type of pilot project for a relatively small group of faculty and students. Identify approximately four faculty members at a given institution judged to have sufficient academic and personal maturity to serve as effective mentors. Assign approximately six freshmen to each of these faculty mentors, with these students chosen on the basis of their potential for academic excellence, and their projected capability for thriving in an educational environment where their academic requirements evolve from the mentor/apprentice relationship rather than following a pre-established pattern. If a college already has an honors program, it is possible that this proposal can be made a part of such a program. The graduation requirements for each student will be individualized and will evolve from the mentor/apprentice relationship, subject to guidelines established by the Academic Policies Committee of the faculty at the particular college. For example, there may be guidelines concerning the balance between breadth and depth of study. During the entire four-year mentorship, this mentoring task will be considered half the faculty member's full-time teaching load. For the purposes of accountability and possible extension of this pilot project, suitable evaluations should be carried out in the senior year to ascertain the effectiveness of this mentoring process, with special emphasis placed on the distinctive goals of Christian higher education.

Increased Emphasis on Study and Dialogue Regarding Fundamental Issues in Philosophy and Theology

> Revise the college program to enable students to develop the philosophical and theological foundation needed as a basis for integrating knowledge across disciplines and forming an integrated Christian conceptual framework.

The most fundamental questions relative to human existence include the following: What is the nature of humanness? What is the nature of the supra-human reality that informs our living as humans? What is of value and what is the nature of moral obligation in light of that which is of value? How does one formulate adequate answers to the above questions? One cannot begin to pursue the tasks of exploring knowledge across disciplines and developing an integrated Christian conceptual framework without first dealing with these fundamental questions. Of course, the reader will recognize that these questions are philosophical (questions of ontology, epistemology, and axiology) as well as theological in nature. This will cause some readers to view this entire proposal as a reflection of the biases of one professional and one amateur philosopher. Therefore, a brief word of defense may be called for. The issue is not whether students ought to deal with these questions. The college student does, in fact, have personal answers to these questions (loosely referred to as a "philosophy of life," or a "world view"), even if these answers are often unsophisticated, incoherent and tacit rather than explicit. The issue is rather whether the student's responses to these questions have been adequately examined and, if needs be, refined in light of criticism and her experience in the world. If we all do indeed have our tacit answers to these questions, then the educational task is to examine and refine those answers, which again is a life-long process, but which calls for initiation at the college level.

If the faculty at a given Christian college share the concerns expressed above, there will obviously be various curricular and co-curricular models for addressing these concerns. However, two observations and related suggestions appear to be somewhat generalizable and appropriate. First, it appears to us that the biblical studies requirements at many Christian colleges are precisely that, without adequate provision for the next logical step, which is to initiate the student into significant theological inquiry and dialogue. Upper level requirements and co-curricular forums should be vehicles for initiating students into such in-depth theological inquiry and dialogue.

The second observation, possibly more idiocyncratic, is our noting of the relative rarity of explicit study requirements in the area of ethics, which deals with the most fundamental questions of moral value and moral obligation. If one accepts the premise that all of life's choices are informed by explicit or tacit value assumptions, then this curricular shortcoming is astounding. It is not unusual for ethical concerns to be incorporated into portions of courses in philosophy and theology, but such tokenism is hardly commensurate with the magnitude of the issues to be studied. It would appear to us that Christian colleges need to place much greater emphasis on the study of ethics.

Of course, if it is true that many students graduate from Christian colleges without having adequately been initiated into the struggle with these fundamental philosophical and theological questions, it is equally true that many of their teachers have not dealt adequately with these questions in a careful and systematic manner. This again points to the immediate need for extensive faculty self-study programs relative to these issues, as already noted in the first proposal above.

Increased Emphasis on Integrative Study in the Senior Year

> Require that approximately one-half of the student's studies
> in the senior year be devoted to integrative themes emphasiz-
> ing the goals of exploring knowledge across disciplines,
> developing an integrated Christian conceptual framework,
> and addressing problems facing the church and the world.

There is a legitimate difference of opinion on Christian college cam-
puses as to whether emphasis on integrative themes should be placed in the
early college years or the upper-level years, or possibly both. One approach
in the early college years is to teach an introductory course that integrates
the insights of philosophy, history and literature. This is a commendable
ideal, provided it indeed reflects integration rather than a placing of disciplines side-by-side by a team of faculty disciplinarians who have not themselves effected an integration. With or without such integrative attempts in
the early college years, our own particular preferences lean toward emphasis on integrative studies in the upper-class years. Our primary reason for
such emphasis is that in-depth integrative study presupposes extensive
foundational studies in various academic disciplines as well as foundational studies relative to the fundamental philosophical and theological questions noted in the proposal presented above. It is our contention that by the
time students reach their senior year they ought to have the foundation necessary for significant initiation into the lifetime integrative task. A number
of Christian colleges do indeed provide such opportunity through capstone
senior seminar courses of an integrative nature. However, it is our observation that such capstone integrative work is only a token portion of a student's total program of study in the senior year. Our proposal is that at least
half of the senior student's study should be devoted to such integrative
themes.

If one accepts this senior year proposal, the type of integrative study
emphasized may be varied, including one or more of the following components: investigation of the underlying philosophical assumptions that
inform the present practice of the students' major discipline; investigation
of a contemporary problem facing the church and/or the world, with an
attempt to bring the insights of various academic disciplines to bear on this
problem; or an attempt to relate the results of scholarship in one or more
academic disciplines to a Christian conceptual framework. The magnitude

of any one of these ventures would suggest the possibility of a significant senior thesis, if not for all students, at least for the most capable (possibly including some of the students involved in the individualized programs of study noted in the earlier proposal for faculty mentoring of students).

We can almost hear the outcry of some Christian college faculty members relative to the sheer magnitude of the proposed integrative studies in the senior year ("half of the student's program of study?"). What of those pre-med students who need all those prescribed science courses in the senior year? What of those many students who come to Christian colleges for reasons other than their primary distinctives as we envision them? Will they put up with such emphasis on these integrative goals during their senior year? Will they go elsewhere where they can receive more traditional career preparation? These are difficult questions. The most courageous answers may suggest that we need to be serious about the distinctives of Christian higher education that cannot be obtained elsewhere. It may be more realistic to suggest that this proposal for the senior year should also be part of a pilot project at some of our Christian colleges, with a possible connection to the pilot project of individualized programs evolving from a faculty/student mentoring relationship. If such a pilot project proves to be effective, then perhaps steps can be taken to generalize it to apply to the entire student body.

Increased Emphasis on Service Internships Integrally Related to Theoretical Study

> Expand the opportunities for students and faculty to take part in service-oriented internships during either the summer or one or both semesters of the academic year, with such internships to be preceded, accompanied, and followed by significant theoretical study and reflection related to the internship activities.

This proposal intends to take seriously the distinctive goal of helping students and faculty develop a sense of responsibility and acquire knowledge for addressing problems facing the church and the world. It is necessary to counteract the myth that college is a detour from living, an interlude of study designed to prepare one for life. Rather, students and faculty need to see more clearly that the biblical concept of truth includes not only the gaining of knowledge, but also the application of such knowledge now, not later.

It is encouraging to note that service-oriented internships are becoming more commonplace as part of the educational experience at Christian colleges. However, it is not unusual for such internships to have rather vague and tenuous connections to any theoretical study preceding, accompanying, or following internship activities. We would strongly urge colleges having or developing such internship programs to pay much greater attention to insuring adequate theoretical study intimately related to internship activities in such a way that there is a constant dialectic between theory and the application of such theory. For example, such internships ought always to be followed by a significant period of reflection about the internship activities, possibly culminating in the writing of a significant paper. Such a paper could be part of the senior thesis idea noted in the proposal immediately above.

Note that our proposal does not limit internship activities to students, but rather encourages faculty also to pursue such activities. The mentoring emphasis in a number of our proposals suggests that faculty and students might cooperate in shared internship activities. This would demonstrate to students that faculty are equally committed to the goal of acquiring knowledge for addressing problems facing the church and the world. Such faculty commitment must be accompanied by administrative support in the form of summer stipends for faculty and the generous awarding of faculty sabbatical leaves and leaves of absence for such purposes.

Refined Student Development Programs that Reflect the Primacy of Learning

Staff responsible for student development programs outside the classroom context need to design these programs to insure that the focus is on learning.

One of the distinctive goals of Christian higher education is to foster non-cognitive development intended to complement the development of cognitive abilities. This legitimate goal often leads to rhetoric about complementing intellectual development with spiritual, social, physical, and emotional development. There is a pernicious tendency to understand commitment to such multiple forms of development to mean that in addition to the primary focus of college education, namely learning, the college ought to foster development in non-cognitive areas that are unrelated to learning. When holistic education is viewed in this way it leads to the college attempting to be all things to all persons by functioning as a church, health spa, and counseling center. We call into question such a compartmentalized view of the aspects of holistic student development. Rather, as a college the primary focus in all activities, both in and out of the classroom, must be on learning. All activities designed to foster non-cognitive development must reflect this common commitment to learning. One simple example may help to clarify this proposal.

An outdated view, in our estimation, of fostering physical development of students in collegiate settings is to require students to take either physical activities courses (courses on individual or dual sports, such as tennis and volleyball) or encouraging students to participate in intramural athletic programs. All too often, such activities are viewed as diversions from college requirements. To be sure, such diversions are necessary but they should not be confused with college education. A more recent focus in the area of physical development is in conformity with the spirit of our proposal. This is to design individual wellness programs for students wherein each student **learns** about the capacities and limitations of her body and is encouraged to make a commitment to caring for herself in ways that comport with such knowledge. These new directions in physical education ought to be applauded. In the spirit of this example, it is our contention that all programs for student development outside of the classroom should be designed to reflect such a primary emphasis on learning. As noted earlier, programs designed primarily for entertainment or diversion value surely have their place in any community, including a college community, but they should not be confused with education.

Reforms in Career Preparation Programs for Employment Upon Graduation

> Evaluate and refine existing programs for career preparation
> in light of the distinctives of Christian liberal arts education.

The truth of the matter is that the majority of students come to Christian liberal arts colleges to prepare for that first job upon graduation, or that series of jobs loosely called a career. Our contention is that if we have only prepared a student for her first job, then we have failed her miserably. On the other hand, preparation for a career involving a succession of jobs with expanding responsibilities has an important place at our colleges, provided great care is taken to insure that this career preparation is congruent with the distinctives of Christian liberal arts education. Experience suggests that such congruence can too easily become the exception rather than the rule.

First, it appears to us that many students plan for a particular career without much critical reflection on the values underlying the practice of that career and whether these values comport with biblical values. We have failed the business major who graduates committed to the individualistic pursuit of a bundle of money without concern for the needs of other people. In contrast, the business major who views her chosen profession as a means for serving others may have caught a glimpse of business as a vocation, a "calling from God." Jesus' call to servanthood is normative for all Christians, not just those in selected professions. Students need squarely to face the question of how their anticipated careers can indeed address problems facing the church and the world. One concrete strategy for such exploration would be a freshman seminar on "Values and Vocation" designed to help students reflect on their value commitments and the nature of biblical values before they choose their major areas of study. This is one partial strategy for our previous suggestion that students need explicit study requirements in the area of ethics, dealing with fundamental questions of moral value and moral obligation.

Attention must also be given to the curricular emphases in existing programs for career preparation. All too often we concentrate on students passively accumulating vast amounts of professional information and techniques without preparing them to interact critically with and transcend this present knowledge, which may soon be obsolete. Our programs for career preparation need to be placed within a program that provides broader perspective. The type of graduate we would want to hire is one who has a good understanding of herself, other persons, social structures, and her natural environment (reflecting breadth of study in the humanities, social sciences and natural sciences); one who has an understanding of important ethical concerns in the given profession; and one who has developed the skills of the broadly educated person. These we take to include the ability to think critically, being able to distinguish true claims to knowledge from false ones; to analyze problem situations, identifying underlying assumptions and proposing effective solutions; to communicate effectively in written and verbal form; and to work effectively with other people in one-on-one or small group settings (all fostered by effective mentor/apprentice relationships while in college). Leaders in industry are telling us that it is the employees with this breadth of knowledge and these skills who advance to positions of major responsibility, not those trapped in the present state of factual information and techniques. Perhaps we are not listening very well.

The implications of the above suggestions are as far-reaching as your imaginations will allow. A few concrete examples may be provocative. A pre-med biology or chemistry major should certainly have a course in medical ethics (even if it means less coverage of material more likely to be on the MCAT exams). A social work major could benefit greatly from an upper-level literature course, with works chosen for their power to illuminate the human condition, even if this means less course coverage of existing social work policy. An education major could benefit from an upper-level course on contemporary problems in education, reading and evaluating the works of recent critics of education, even if this means one less course in pedagogy. And business majors could benefit from a senior-level case-studies course, having a course in business ethics as a prerequisite; or a course in decision-making that draws on sources from psychology, sociology and literature, even if this means one less course on existing principles of management. By now you get the idea.

Of course, a common critique of the above suggestions, already hinted at, is that since the prescription of credit requirements for undergraduate majors appears to be a zero-sum game, the addition of this "fluff" will necessitate reduction of the "real stuff." Students wanting the "real stuff" will simply go elsewhere for their undergraduate education.

Two responses are possible. The first is to reiterate the message from industry leaders that the critics may have the "fluff" and the "real stuff" backwards. A second response is to suggest a more modest approach of incorporating broader educational emphases into curricula designed to make possible immediate postgraduate employment. This would mean refining existing courses in more reflective and critical directions rather than creating new courses. The catch is that the faculty and student critics will no doubt also resist this more modest venture as "lacking relevance." The potential faculty resistance is the most disturbing. It can be addressed in the long run only by increasing breadth in the education of future generations of college teachers in the disciplines oriented to immediate postgraduate employment.

Governing Board and Administrative Support of all Agenda Items Noted Above

> The governing boards and administrations of colleges intending to be serious about the distinctives of Christian higher education must realign their priorities to make possible programs of the type noted above, including the allocation of significant funds for such programs.

It is our experience that the types of innovative programs noted above do not generally meet with enthusiastic support from the governing boards and administrations of Christian colleges. There is a tendency for such authorities to slant Christian higher education primarily in the direction of traditional preparation for employment, thereby giving short shrift to programs designed to implement the goals that are distinctive for such education. Few of the proposals noted above will get off the ground without significant funding, which will necessitate a major shift in the present priorities of many persons working at the administrative and governing board levels.

To be more specific, the programs noted above cannot be viewed as additional responsibilities for faculty members already carrying a full load of traditional responsibilities. Both of us lived through (somehow!) an experience wherein an innovative team-taught interdisciplinary senior seminar which required an enormous time commitment was accepted by a college administration only under the provision that all teachers involved teach such a course over and above their normal teaching loads. This reflected an unambiguous priority judgment on the part of the administration of that college which clearly conflicted with the distinctive goals of Christian higher education.

The types of programs proposed above suggest that an important area for establishing funding priorities is faculty learning and development. The view that faculty members hired to teach at Christian colleges have already arrived will not wash. They have barely begun their own educations once their formal degree work is done, if they intend to be serious about the distinctive goals we have discussed. Therefore, much greater emphasis must be placed on continual faculty growth and development as older learners who grow together with the younger learners they mentor.

A PROPOSED NEW MODEL FOR CHRISTIAN HIGHER EDUCATION

In addition to the agenda set forth above for existing Christian liberal arts colleges, we turn to a proposal for a radically new model for Christian higher education that hopefully will stimulate criticism and provoke alternative proposals. Our model places emphasis on educating future teachers for Christian colleges or future Christian teachers who wish to serve at secular colleges and universities. It is our judgment that current means for educating this population are inadequate in that they do not sufficiently emphasize deep philosophical and theological understanding; they do not prepare future teachers to deal with the most fundamental assumptions underlying the practice of their respective disciplines; and they do not address strategies for developing Christian perspectives on learning within the respective academic disciplines. Under present models, these emphases are seldom directly addressed during the future teacher's formal education, leaving the teacher the unreasonable task of "catching up" while teaching.

Since we have gone that route ourselves, we know how inhuman it is. A new model must be developed wherein such emphases are primary within the formal education of these future college teachers, prior to their first teaching assignments.

It should be noted that although the proposed model will emphasize foundational studies in theology and philosophy, and the study of foundational academic disciplines (e.g., economics, rather than business; sociology rather than social work), we firmly believe that this model will provide the best foundation even for students preparing to become college teachers in the more applied, career-oriented undergraduate areas. We would encourage such students to pursue their professional studies at the graduate level (e.g., a doctoral program in social work built on an undergraduate major in sociology or psychology; an MBA program built on an undergraduate major in economics). Students pursuing this new model will be well-prepared to address the need to incorporate a broader perspective into their future teaching of undergraduate career-oriented majors.

As a final note, although our proposed new model is primarily designed with future college teachers in mind, it is our contention that Phase I of our proposal is equally well suited to serious undergraduate students who wish to develop the best possible foundation for rigorous professional studies and are willing to postpone more career oriented professional studies until after their undergraduate experience. Our proposal for a new model consists of three phases.

PHASE I: AMBROSE HOUSE—The Residential Undergraduate College Affiliated With an Existing Christian Liberal Arts College

Ambrose House[8] will be a residential undergraduate college, serving approximately fifty students who will live together in a residence hall located on or near the campus of an existing Christian liberal arts college. The faculty of Ambrose House will consist of twelve resident fellows having offices in the same residence hall, which will also have adequate classroom and seminar room facilities.

---

[8] After the teacher of St. Augustine, for (we hope) obvious reasons.

The academic specializations of the faculty resident fellows will cover the following twelve areas, with one fellow specializing in each area: philosophy, theology, literature, art or music or theatre, psychology, sociology, economics, political science, biology, chemistry, physics, mathematics. Undergraduate students will be selected such that each resident fellow is mentor to four undergraduates pursuing an academic specialization in her area for that academic year.

Ambrose House will accept students who have excelled in their high school academic work, who have an interest in future vocations as college teachers and who demonstrate the potential for excellence as Christian teachers and scholars at the college or university level, or who wish to pursue rigorous foundational studies prior to professional studies at the graduate level. Entrance requirements will insure that each admitted student has demonstrated adequate quantitative, reading and writing skills prior to matriculation. The program of Ambrose House will be administered by a director who will hold an administrative appointment at the affiliated college. The resident faculty fellows will hold appointments as faculty members of the affiliated college and the students of Ambrose House will be considered a part of the student body of the college. The curriculum as well as all policies and procedures pertaining to implementation will be determined by the faculty resident fellows, subject to the approval of the affiliated college. Performance evaluations for faculty shall be conducted in accordance with expectations and procedures agreed upon with the affiliated college.

All students of Ambrose House shall be eligible to enroll in regular college courses offered by the affiliated college, in accordance with the personal educational plan developed for each student in consultation with her faculty mentor. Each student will be expected to meet the following requirements for 32 courses during a four-year program: (a) completion of a core curriculum offered at Ambrose House, consisting of 18 courses (listed below); (b) completion of 10 courses in a chosen academic specialization, with such courses taken either at the parent college or by means of independent study under the faculty mentor; and (c) completion of four courses in one or both of the major divisions of knowledge other than that division in which a student is specializing (the three major divisions of knowledge being the arts and humanities, the natural sciences, and the social sciences). This is to be done in accordance with one of the following two patterns: a four-course sequence in one academic discipline in one of these two divisions; or a two-course sequence in one academic discipline in each of two divisions of knowledge.

With the exception of the prescribed core curriculum courses required of all Ambrose House students, the remainder of each student's program of study will be individually designed on the basis of consultation between the student and her mentor, with the final program of study to be approved by the faculty mentor. In addition to pursuing this four-year program of study during the regular academic years, students will be strongly encouraged by faculty mentors to pursue elective courses in established summer school programs or additional independent study in elective areas during the summer months.

The Core Curriculum

First Year: Intellectual History I, II
Introduction to Biblical & Theological Studies
Biblical Theology
Christian Perspectives I: The Arts & Humanities
Christian Perspectives II: The Natural Sciences &
    Mathematics

Second Year: Epistemology
Axiology & Ethics
Theological Issues
Christian Perspectives III: The Social Sciences

Third Year: Ontology
Comparative World Views
Christianity and Contemporary Issues I

Fourth Year: Integrative Seminar in the Academic Specialization
Integrative Senior Thesis in the Academic Specialization
    (3 courses)
Christianity & Contemporary Issues II

The Christianity and Contemporary Issues sequence shall include exploration of the interrelationships between theoretical and praxis-oriented scholarship, emphasizing applications of the student's major. For example, a student specializing in Sociology may explore implications of her specialization for the criminal justice system. Or a student majoring in Philosophy may explore contemporary issues in medical ethics. During the summer between the two courses in this sequence, each student will participate in a field experience enabling her to apply theoretical understanding to problems facing an appropriate needy population.

In addition to the above formal requirements, each student at Ambrose House will be expected to pursue an individualized non-credit program that fosters personal well-being throughout her four years of residence. These supervised programs shall emphasize both learning and practice relative to physical and emotional wellness, including attention to individualized exercise programs and nutrition.

As a complement to these individualized wellness programs, more informal opportunities will be provided for fostering caring relationships between members of the Ambrose House community, for individual and corporate worship, and for actively serving the local community.

PHASE II: The Post-Doctoral Year at Ambrose House

Christian scholars who have just completed doctoral programs shall be eligible to apply for a post-doctoral year at Ambrose House, with special preference given to candidates committed to pursuing college or university teaching positions. The educational background of all applicants should include the type of philosophical, theological and integrative studies background provided by the undergraduate program at Ambrose House, and first priority for acceptance into the post-doctoral program will eventually be given to graduates of the Ambrose House program.

Each post-doctoral scholar shall have an academic specialization corresponding to a specialization of one of the twelve faculty resident fellows. At any point in time, each resident fellow shall be responsible for mentoring a maximum of two post-doctoral scholars, in addition to the four undergraduate students being mentored.

The program of study for a post-doctoral scholar shall be individually designed, based on conversations between the scholar and her mentor. Emphasis will be placed on the development of Christian perspectives on learning, with particular emphasis on synthesis of the results of the student's undergraduate foundational Christian studies with the results of her doctoral studies. The only specific requirement will be that each post-doctoral student shall write one major paper, worthy of consideration for publication in a scholarly journal, which shall be presented to a meeting of the entire Ambrose House community.

PHASE III: The Visiting Research Fellows Program at Ambrose House

The total program at Ambrose House shall place significant emphasis on research activities for faculty resident fellows, not as a substitute for teaching, but rather as an indispensable complement to teaching. It is necessary for Christian scholars to have sufficient time to produce quality scholarly publications for dissemination to the larger academic community. The fact that each faculty resident fellow will be mentoring approximately six students at any one time (four undergraduate students and two post-doctoral scholars) will make it possible for the resident fellow to devote significant time to research and publication activities. Each faculty resident fellow shall have access to the library and research facilities of the affiliated college.

As a complement to and further extension of the work of the faculty resident fellows, Ambrose House shall also sponsor a Visiting Research Fellows Program. Under this program, Christian scholars from any college or university shall be eligible for a full-time appointment of from one to three years duration. Appointments will be made on a competitive basis, with participants to be chosen by a committee consisting of the director of Ambrose House and faculty resident fellows. The major criteria for appointment as a visiting research fellow shall be the applicant's potential for the production of significant scholarly or other creative work and the potential benefits of interaction between the fellow and the rest of the Ambrose House community.

At any point in time, there shall be a maximum of six visiting research fellows on appointment, with appointments to be made without reference to their academic specializations. Research projects for visiting research fellows may either be individual projects or group projects dealing with selected interdisciplinary themes.

The research projects to be pursued by visiting research fellows shall focus on the development of Christian perspectives on learning. Such projects may deal with issues within a given academic discipline, with issues of an interdisciplinary nature, or with contemporary issues of a theoretical or/and practical nature that are especially relevant to the church and to the redemptive witness of the church in the world.

Visiting research fellows shall not have specific teaching assignments during their terms of appointment. However, they shall be expected to interact with appropriate faculty resident fellows as well as post-doctoral fellows and undergraduate students by means of periodic individual meetings, small seminar sessions and informal discussions.

Ambrose House: Prelude or Alternative to a Major Christian University?

There has been some discussion in recent years about the possibility of establishing a major Christian university within the evangelical tradition. Some reflections are in order concerning the relationship between the model we propose above and such a future possibility.

As noted in Chapter 3, there are some present models for Christian education through the doctorate level in selected academic disciplines, such as psychology and philosophy. To extend such education to a comprehensive list of academic specializations through a Christian university model might appear to be a laudable ideal, especially in light of the fact that the prevailing paradigms for study and research in many academic disciplines at secular universities are not informed by philosophical and theological presuppositions that are congruent with the Christian faith. However, we believe there are two inter-related difficulties with this university vision, at least at the present state in the evolution of Christian higher education.

First, there seems to be an ever-present dangerous tendency for Christians to speak only to one another relative to important academic issues, not to mention other issues. This too often leads to a sort of tribalism and Christian ghetto mentality that does not lend itself to a strong Christian witness in the world. A related difficulty is that centers for Christian scholarship may presently be viewed as marginal by the greater academic community since the prevailing paradigms in many disciplines are not informed by presuppositions congruent with the Christian faith.

To create models viewed as marginal by the larger academic community is detrimental to our witness to that community. Rather, our belief that scholarship informed by Christian presuppositions makes the greatest sense of human experience is best expressed through models wherein such Christian scholarship receives a hearing in the greater academic market place. Therefore, a central aspect of the model we propose is encouragement of active person-to-person dialogue between Christian scholars and scholars holding different sets of presuppositions. This type of emphasis is built into our proposed model by means of the obvious progression from foundational undergraduate Christian studies within a Christian community to in-depth doctoral studies at leading secular universities, followed by further post-doctoral reflections on the development of Christian perspectives on all learning and the production of sound scholarship that will have an impact on the entire world community of learners. In this way, Christian scholars will truly be the salt and light they are called to be within the larger academic community.

If the Ambrose House model is implemented with excellence, it could contribute to the increased dissemination of Christian scholarship that may be a necessary precondition for funding a major Christian university in North America. Another possible transition model toward establishing such a university is provided by the examples of Conrad Grebel College and the Psychological Studies Institute presented in Chapter 3, in which a satellite Christian college is affiliated or federated with a secular university. This involves collaborative programs of study involving faculty with joint appointments leading to undergraduate or graduate degrees awarded by the university, with adequate means established to create dialogue between members of the satellite college and other segments of the university.

Having said this, however, we can still envision the eventual development of a major Christian university in North America at such a time when scholarship from a Christian perspective has gained a greater hearing within the various academic disciplines. Of course, we would argue that the focus of the curriculum for such a Christian university ought to be on increased depth of accomplishment of the five major distinctives of Christian higher education. It could even be argued that the undergraduate curriculum at such a university ought to be similar to the curriculum we propose for Phase I of Ambrose House, with more specialized career preparation and professional training to take place at the graduate level. In any case, unless the distinctives of Christian higher education are given full priority in practice, any actual attempt at creating a Christian university would be a profligate waste of the Christian community's resources.

NOTES ON CHAPTER 4

For a previous summary statement of our Ambrose House proposal, see Harold Heie, "Wanted: Christian Colleges for a Dynamic Evangelicalism," *Christian Scholar's Review* XXI:3, March 1992, pp. 254-274.

For an excellent series of essays on the history and mission of Christian colleges in America, see *Making Higher Education Christian*, edited by Joel A. Carpenter and Kenneth W. Shipps (Grand Rapids: Christian University Press, 1987). Of particular relevance to our proposal are the essays by Nathan O. Hatch, "Evangelical Colleges and the Challenge of Christian Thinking"; Richard J. Mouw, "Knowing and Doing: The Christian College in Contemporary Society"; and George M. Marsden, "Why No Major Evangelical University? The Loss and Recovery of Evangelical Advanced Scholarship". In his essay, Marsden argues that "Rather than attempting to surmount the formidable obstacles to the founding of a full-fledged university, . . . [evangelicals] should establish a number of high quality research institutes. . . . In this way, the real goals of an evangelical research university — penetrating the highest level of the critical thought of culture and offering thoroughly Christian wisdom for public application — could be accomplished, and accomplished soon." (pp. 301,303). The second and third phases of our proposed Ambrose House constitute one model for promoting such quality research from a Christian perspective.

In a more recent publication, Marsden adds another strategy to the proposal noted above. See George M. Marsden, "The Soul of the American University: A Historical Overview," in George M. Marsden and Bradley J. Longfield, editors, *The Secularization of the Academy* (New York: Oxford University Press, 1992), pp. 9-45. In this essay, Marsden reiterates the strategy of "building research and graduate study centers in key fields at the best institutions in various Christian sub-cultures" (p.41). But he also proposes the additional strategy that "serious religious people begin to campaign actively for universities to apply their professions of pluralism more consistently" (p.38), fully recognizing that this second strategy may not be as realistic as the first strategy (p. 41).

In brief, Marsden's argument for this second strategy is that "if public places such as our major universities are going to operate on the premise that moral judgments are relative to communities, then we should follow the implications of that premise as consistently as we can and not absolutize one or perhaps a few sets of opinions and exclude all others. In other words, our pluralism should attempt to be more consistently inclusive, embracing even traditional Christian views" (p.38). Marsden suggests that one way for universities consistently to apply their premise of pluralism is for them "to conceive of themselves as federations for competing intellectual communities of faith or commitment" (p.40). Noting that this strategy "might be more difficult for American universities than for British or some Canadian universities, which have always seen themselves as federations of colleges among which there was sometimes diversity. American schools, by contrast, were shaped first by sectarian Christian and then by Enlightenment and liberal Protestant ideals that assumed that everyone ought to think alike" (p.40), Marsden nevertheless concludes that "if American schools were willing to recognize diversity and perhaps even to incorporate colleges with diverse commitments, whether religious, feminist, gay, politically conservative, humanist, liberationist, or whatever, pluralism might have a better chance" (pp.40,41). Of the various models reported on in this volume, the satellite Christian college examples of Conrad Grebel College and the Psychological Studies Institute bear some resemblance to Marsden's proposed second strategy. However, we would argue that if a university dares to create a federation for "competing intellectual communities of faith or commitment," these competing communities should not just co-exist. Rather, such diversity can be a vehicle for our learning from one another only if steps are taken to facilitate dialogue.

CHAPTER 5

IS REFORM REALLY FEASIBLE?
A DIALOGUE

That evening two weeks before with Dean Zufrieden and Professor Verbessern had not exactly left me hungering for more. My acquaintances had both left frustrated and sullen. I had embarrassed myself several times and had no desire to repeat the performance. What had promised to be stimulating had turned out, I thought, a flop.

I was therefore all the more surprised when both Verbessern and Zufrieden called me in the same afternoon and suggested we all get together again. Zufrieden informed me that he had had a wonderful time and could hardly wait to get at Verbessern to discuss Christian higher education again.

His reasons soon became clear, however, when I discovered that Verbessern had been recommending a book which urged reform of Christian college priorities and proposed an experimental program to be tried at an existing Christian college. Zufrieden now had studied ideas in print which Verbessern endorsed, analyzed them and was, as they say, "loaded for bear."

Reluctantly, I agreed to a rematch. This time I had resigned myself to being a good listener and referee, which seemed less likely to result in loss of face and decorum on my part. The evening was chosen, and once again I was to play host.

As we settled into the same chairs as that earlier night, I noticed a difference in the atmosphere. It was warmer weather, so there was no friendly fire crackling in the fireplace. Even the rich aroma of Verbessern's pipe was missing. The pipe and tobacco pouch lay in the open briefcase at his feet. He sat rather stiff and braced in a chair that should have encouraged a relaxed posture.

Zufrieden on the other hand was cheerful and animated. He carried a copy of the book which Verbessern had recommended. In a chance glimpse I noticed that some pages of the book were heavily underlined and had notations in the margins. I became increasingly uneasy.

"Well, shall we begin?" blurted out Zufrieden. I had hoped for some friendly preliminary conversation, but that seemed to have been overruled.

"Verbessern, my friend, I am surprised at the number of good ideas you have endorsed in this slim volume," began Zufrieden, gesturing with the book in question. "Let me be specific. The ideas of increasing the emphasis and funding of faculty study and research programs, programs that involve integrative work, are just excellent. The idea of older or more experienced faculty mentoring younger faculty on integrative themes, that's even better. Granted that this would have to be worked out in terms of the way in which funding is allocated, I agree with you one hundred percent that we have to make good on our claims that Christian distinctives are our highest priorities. And I could not agree more with the notion of bringing service internships and student development into line with the primacy of learning. The ideas about the integration of our religious commitments with both theoretical and practical concerns are first rate stuff!

"However," said Zufrieden, after a long and very meaningful pause, "I still have some reservations about other features in the proposal." Here Zufrieden wrinkled his forehead as if in intense concentration; a gesture that always was impressive to those who knew the care with which he formulated his criticisms. "Certain things I feel I am morally bound as both a Christian and a scholar to raise about this proposal. In the first place, the idea of attaching the pilot or model program to an existing liberal arts college has serious problems. I realize, of course, that it has practical and strategic advantages with respect to available facilities. It would provide a broader range of subjects available for the students to study than if you just created a pilot program from scratch. Yet I am very concerned about what kind of an impact the presence of such a program, including the students and faculty of that program, would have on the existing institution.

"It seems to me that it is, at the very least, an elitist proposal. The faculty in the existing institution are going to have serious and perhaps legitimate complaints about the very different work load and salaries, possibly, of the faculty in the experimental program. Students in the regular college are going to look upon the students in the experimental college as kind of weird and kooky. They are going to think of them as egg-heads, while the students in the experimental program are going to look down upon the students at the more traditional school as purely job oriented in their interests, as somehow seeking an inferior kind of Christian education. It just seems to me that we would be asking for serious trouble by doing this.

"I would be most interested, Verbessern, in hearing what kind of response you might give to the practicality of setting up such an experimental college at an existing Christian college. I have some serious theoretical questions that I would like to raise, but let's be practical at the outset. Even setting financial questions aside, presuming that there are enough people who believe, as we do, that the money we spend on Christian higher education must be spent supporting the priorities that we claim. Even assuming that, shouldn't we be working to strengthen existing Christian colleges rather than grafting on troublesome experimental programs of this sort?"

As Zufrieden spoke he became increasingly intense in his manner, leaned far forward in his seat and as he completed his criticism remained poised, his eyes boring deeply into Verbessern, as he anticipated the response.

Verbessern, who had been sitting on the edge of his chair, heaved a very deep sigh and leaned back. I couldn't tell whether the sigh was a sigh of relief that the criticism had not been as bad as he had anticipated. Or whether it was a sigh recognizing that the worst had come to pass, and that indeed this was something that Verbessern had worried about and did not have an adequate answer for. There was a period of silence as he sat apparently staring into space, forming, I hoped, an answer. I was on the verge of offering to get refreshments because the silence had gone on so long, when Verbessern cleared his throat, refocused his eyes, and began to speak.

"Well," he began slowly and thoughtfully, "the charge of elitism in Christian higher education is not new. Your own institution, Zufrieden, which prides itself in the excellence of its program has often been charged with elitism.

"You yourself, I've heard it, have articulated the classic defense of excellence. It is that excellence keeps alive what is best; and excellence produces leadership without which everything falls into mediocrity. So in principle, at least, there is no sound argument against a program or a college that strives to do excellently or even adequately what all of the colleges claim should be their first priority.

"Now, it seems to me that in any situation when faced with a challenge, it is possible for those who are challenged to respond in one of two ways. One can either refuse the challenge, belittle the challenger, demean the principles that lie behind the challenge, become withdrawn and defensive of the status quo. Or one can rise to the challenge and benefit from the rigor that the challenge imposes. The presence of the proposed program on a traditional campus is just such a challenge to that campus itself.

"But if by elitist what you really mean is that this is not an educational program that is appropriate for everyone, then you are absolutely right. It is not for everyone any more than everyone should be a physics major, or a philosophy major, or a literature major. That doesn't make those majors elitist. But certainly the program that is proposed in the book is not for everyone. It is a special purpose program given the current state of Christian higher education. As such it does meet a pressing need. We need in our Christian colleges faculty members who know what they are doing in relating their faith to their disciplines, who have the benefit from the ground up in their undergraduate experience of integrating faith, and learning, and practice."

"Now hold on just a moment right there," interrupted Zufrieden, leaning forward once again. He had settled back to listen to Verbessern's response. Zufrieden had spent the entire time of Verbessern's little discourse leaning back in his chair with his thumbs and little fingers together, tapping his middle fingers rhythmically against one another. "I accept your response to the elitist criticism. I have long myself contended that there are various sorts of education possible, appropriate to various sorts of career needs. And suppose I were to admit that those who were specifically interested in lives of scholarship and teaching could benefit from a more high powered program than most of our Christian liberal arts colleges offer.

" Still it seems to me that what you are doing constitutes a fairly explicit criticism of our existing liberal arts college programs, since many of them do say they are preparing their students for careers of scholarship and college teaching. Sometimes there are even honors programs which permit the more capable students to move at a faster rate, enriching their educational experience. So at the very least it seems to me that though you may not be elitist in any sense that doesn't already exist in Christian higher education, nevertheless you certainly are launching a criticism against existing programs in this respect."

Towards the end of his question, Zufrieden let his voice become a little more tentative and a little less strident. It seems to me that he was beginning already to see the answer to his own objection.

Verbessern, rather than allowing the conversation to lapse into reflective thought, took advantage of Zufrieden's trailing uncertainty at the end of his remarks and jumped right in. "Well of course. This whole proposal is a result of a sympathetic criticism of current Christian higher education. In that sense, then, its very existence as an alternative is an embodied criticism of current practice. But once again, that can be seen as either a negative consequence of the proposal or a positive one. It seems to me that a proposal that has been formulated to meet existing needs and deficits can serve as a challenge to the other programs that have those deficits.

"So I don't see that what you have said is so much an objection as a statement of the problem. Yes, we have criticized existing Christian higher education, and yes, this is a proposal in the face of those criticisms. Therefore, the proposal does imply a criticism of the existing programs, insofar as they claim to be producing Christian scholars and teachers.

"Now it is also true that if the faculty in Christian colleges had the sort of undergraduate experience that is proposed in this book, they would be better equipped to do for all students, regardless of their career plans, what we claim to be doing in our catalogs. So, yes, I suppose it is also a criticism of the level of preparedness that we have been able to achieve on the part of faculties in Christian colleges. And this is not, obviously, a criticism of the individuals themselves, so much as it is a criticism of the system in which we educate those who become our faculty. Most of us have experienced those deficits and know how hard it is necessary to work to overcome them. We have seen people who have enormous difficulty overcoming them because they lack the early training in conceptual thought and reflection on their disciplines that allows them to bring theological ideas to bear on their work."

Zufrieden was silent for a moment and seemed to be reorganizing his thoughts a little. He stared thoughtfully into space for a few moments. One of the things I always liked about these encounters was the freedom that participants had to think between various phases of the discussion. One could always simply reflect for a few minutes, and no silence was ever embarrassing to the participants, a true mark of gentlemen who wished to pursue truth rather than win strategic advantage. In spite of that fact I also recognized that emotions ran quite high in some of these matters.

Finally Zufrieden seemed to have reorganized himself and said to Verbessern, "One last thing on the practical side of this before I raise another kind of question. What about 'inbreeding'? At least for the foreseeable future a program of this sort is going to exist at only one or a very few schools. That means that we're going to be flooding our undergraduate programs at some point in the future with teachers all of whom have had identical undergraduate experience. Ahh.... Isn't that a problem?"

Verbessern did not pause even for a moment in responding to Zufrieden, as if he had thought about this objection at length and had anticipated that it would be raised. And he pulled a strategy that I saw him using on Zufrieden any number of times, when he said, "Now wait a moment. Inbreeding is a term that covers quite a variety of things. For example suppose I were proposing a program in which from their undergraduate years students went all the way through to take their doctoral work without any exposure outside of our system. And then suppose we sent all of them out to teach in Christian schools, and the next generation of teachers did the same thing, especially if they in turn became the teachers at our school. Then surely that would be a most serious type of inbreeding. But I think that it is pretty obvious from the proposal that's not what is being suggested.

"In your own school a large number of the faculty have undergraduate degrees from that school. In fact you are an alumnus. Now you know exactly what your defense against the charge of inbreeding is in a case like that. All of you have taken advanced degrees at first rate universities here and abroad. So that while the undergraduate program in principle is supposed to give you a good base for relating your faith to your discipline, the graduate training exposes you to a variety of different schools of thought, a variety of different ideas and approaches. So since we expect our students to do exactly that, our claim is only that we are doing what others claim they are doing. But we are actually going to do it, and we are going to do it well. So I don't see that the charge of inbreeding applies to our program any more than it applies to any of the existing Christian colleges."

Zufrieden made a small gesture with his hand that indicated that he saw the point, accepted it and wished to go on to other matters. Here there was a brief interruption, because my wife came into the living room and said, "Pardon me gentlemen, but there is hot coffee available in the kitchen." She looked at me and said, "Honey, if you don't mind, would you be willing to slip out and bring that in along with the donuts that are out there?"

I said I would and slipped out of the room. After I had organized everything on a tray, which I had a little difficulty finding, I brought the whole business in, only to discover that while I was gone the conversation had taken off anew. And as I quietly came into the room and placed the coffee and donuts on the coffee table, I found that Verbessern and Zufrieden and my wife were in a heated argument. This time I found I had missed the beginning, but where I picked it up it was going something like this.

Zufrieden had just finished saying something that I didn't quite catch. Verbessern was leaning back in his chair with his eyes closed and his hands folded over his chest. And my wife was just saying, "Of course I agree with you that all Christian higher education is based on religious and philosophical and value commitments. But I don't agree that this implies we ought to have a Christian university with graduate programs through the doctoral level."

To this Zufrieden reacted immediately and said, "Don't you see that if we really were to believe as Verbessern does, and I do, and you do, that if education is never neutral, and if what we want are the very best prepared Christian scholars, then some sort of a Christian paradigm ought to be the working model for every Christian's education and research, especially if we are talking about scholars who are capable of working at the cutting edge of their disciplines.

"Given this logic, I don't see how it is possible to avoid the conclusion that Verbessern here should have proposed a Christian university rather than a program, an undergraduate program, that is attached to an existing Christian college. Why not overturn the whole system and make the radical proposal of the Christian university? After all, why should it be that a Christian who is capable of doing first rate research based on his Christian presuppositions should spend years in a secular university where his research is going to be based on the presuppositions of non-Christian advisors. She'll have to do that because in order for her doctoral research to pass the department it has to be acceptable to those scholars.

"Can't you see that this is a logical extension of the argument for reform? I'm saying Verbessern has not gone far enough." And with this outburst, Zufrieden rose from his chair, walked over to the tray, picked up a cup of coffee, doctored it to his taste, went back and sat down to listen to the response.

Verbessern opened his eyes and looked a little uncertain about what he was to say. Apparently Zufrieden's argument that he had not been radical enough and that his premises implied a much more extensive program, had in fact struck home. "Well," Verbessern began a little uncertainly, "uh, it seems to me that you may be right that eventually the ideal would be a Christian university. But, uh, it seemed that was not a practical idea right now. I think perhaps this should be seen as a pilot program which if successful could be expanded into a Christian university. It will be a model of what ought to be done at the undergraduate level in such a university or perhaps supply teachers for that kind of a school in the future."

My wife, however, turned and looked at Verbessern aghast, as if she could not believe that she was hearing him say that. "Now," she said, "just a moment. I don't think you should cave in to that criticism so fast. For one thing, if you're worried about inbreeding and a kind of ghetto mentality then it seems to me that you would surely end up with it, if you were talking about the Christian university. I don't see that it would ever be possible for us to have more than one major, really major, first-rate Christian university in this country. This means that everybody who's anybody has got to go through it and out to teach at Christian schools, and it will be hiring its own graduates as faculty. I mean, that's the worst case that you were just talking about. Talk about tribal mentality! You're going to have an isolationist academic community that we have been working our way out of for years, ever since some unaccredited schools gave Ph.D.'s to people who then were hired to teach at the same university."

Well, Verbessern was a bit taken aback at the speed and vehemence of her comeback. He made as if to say something, but without breaking stride she continued. "Look, one of the important strengths of what you have proposed is that students who are well prepared in their undergraduate training then go out and enter into dialogue with paradigms and faculty at major universities.

"That's a real advantage because it gives them the opportunity to see from the inside what is going on at these other schools, including what is going on in research. So when they come back to teach at Christian colleges they have a first-hand, experiential appreciation for what their colleagues at the secular schools are doing. Furthermore, it gives them an opportunity to witness to their faith in the larger academic community. It allows people out there to see that there are Christian scholars who are able to do excellent work, but are still committed to seeing things from a Christian perspective.

"Surely one of the things you ought to be doing," she said turning to Verbessern again, "is to prepare the students who are going on to these universities to know how to handle themselves well. They need to know how to optimize their witness in the academic community, without resorting to street corner type evangelism and without making themselves appear foolish. Any conceivable advantage that the Christian university might have seems to me to be provided by the post-doctoral year and Visiting Research Fellows Program. There you have people who have done their doctoral work and have come back for a year in a kind of internship in the new program, working closely with the senior mentors, as well as having an opportunity to devote primary energy to advanced Christian scholarship.

"So I fail to see any real advantage to the Christian university. It would create a much more protected environment, and it would have higher visibility as the world counts visibility. So you could have winning basketball teams and football teams and that sort of thing, and major research being done, perhaps, right at your university. But those are of considerably more peripheral importance than to produce fine Christian scholars who have been exposed to the world's learning and who have been a witness in the context of the academic give and take of a major university. They could come back and consolidate their thinking under mature Christian scholars and then go out and teach at major universities or in our Christian colleges.

"I think we would be inviting a quiet revolution of competence in these matters for our faculties. I think that existing faculty in Christian colleges could only benefit from having people like this joining them. All of us know how much we learn from our colleagues, and surely I would find it enormously stimulating to have someone like that joining a faculty where I taught."

Verbessern spread his hands in concession. Zufrieden was a little startled by the turn of the conversation since he hadn't planned on this fourth participant. I stood in the doorway where I had started to go back out to the kitchen and smiled quietly to myself.

There was a period while everyone kind of digested the arguments that had been thrown back and forth. Finally, Zufrieden looked up from his coffee and said, "Well, maybe you have something, Verbessern." Verbessern looked up from stirring his coffee and said, "Perhaps I have."

My wife said, "What do you mean, 'maybe'?"

I cleared my throat and said, "Donuts anyone?"

EPILOGUE: SERPENTS AND DOVES

We earnestly hope that the rabbit is not really dead. The slogans which have become dear to the rhetoric of Christian higher education are in reality a powerful system of ideas that contains a vision of education with which many of us have fallen in love. It has the potential, given proper structures and caring mentors, to help our Christian youth to become (to change to a biblical metaphor) as wise as serpents and as harmless as doves.

Serpents, like foxes, are sometimes used as a symbol of cleverness, though at least in the biblical literature they are not usually portrayed as especially good models of virtue. We are not so sure about doves. Sometimes they are symbolic of the Holy Spirit, but often they are just examples of gentle creatures. As to their intelligence, that is what we are not so sure about. But if they are no brighter than the ducks waddling around outside the barn where this is being written, then they don't win any awards in the wisdom category.

We have sometimes been effective at making our students as wise as serpents, but often have not done very much to prevent them from being as harmful as serpents. A Christian psychological therapist told us with evident concern that she had encountered a number of the graduates of one of our better integrative programs. Though well trained and academically prepared, they seemed more concerned with their hourly rates than with sacrificial service. There is little of the dove in preoccupation with wealth and luxurious lifestyle. Christian education must be about developing a sense of responsibility for addressing the problems facing the world and the church, in a word "service."

On the other hand, we have sometimes encouraged our students to be as harmless as doves, but have done this by so preoccupying their undergraduate years with facts and the details of career preparation that they never had to wrestle with the tough issues that will make them as wise as serpents. Wisdom without service is empty; service without wisdom is blind. (Apologies to Immanuel Kant)

In our opinion the key to genuinely Christian education is the close working relation of a mentor and a student. Assuming a degree of Christian maturity on the part of the mentor, this is our best shot at nurturing the

dove in our students. It is not apt to happen in mass produced education; it is somewhat more likely to happen in a caring relationship between a master and an apprentice. "Better caught than taught" still applies.

Assuming a degree of scholarly maturity on the part of the mentor, this is our best shot at nurturing the **serpent** in our students. Surface facts of a discipline can be recited to an audience of hundreds with some success; the inner workings of a scholarly discipline or creative process can only be shown to a small number of intimate disciples. The best teachers and the brightest students already know this, but they often have to work outside of or against our present educational structures to take advantage of this insight.

This sort of thinking goes against all the current business models for running a cost-effective college program, but it is exactly what needs to be done. To repeat a point made earlier, not all things in life need to be justified by the pragmatic principle of whether it will pay for itself. Neither our pets nor our children could conceivably meet that criterion. Nevertheless, it seems to us that the mentor/student relationship is at the heart of Christian education. Without this component everything else limps along, at best. Until we are willing to bite the bullet on this one, we will probably be stuck with placing bandaids on old programs.

Probably the most important resource upon which we will have to draw, if we are to undertake reform of Christian higher education, has yet to be mentioned. It is our courage. Reform always involves risk for the simple reason that the new structures are untested. "If it's not broke, don't fix it" is the adage of everyone who opposes change, and a case can nearly always be made that something is not broken quite badly enough to justify the effort required to fix it. Our proposal is that Christian higher education is not broken, but often solemnly wrong-headed. Its priorities simply do not match the claims by which it justifies its existence. It isn't what it pretends to be, rather like good old Puzzle in the lion skin in C. S. Lewis's *The Last Battle*. He was a donkey pretending to be a lion, a good and gentle donkey, to be sure, even a brave and unexpectedly resourceful donkey, but definitely not a lion.

Unlike Puzzle, however, Christian higher education can become what it claims to be by an outstanding exercise in courage and creativity. Where can we get the courage? Many of us have endured notable economic hardships, personal sacrifice, overwork and stress in order to participate in the dream of Christian higher education. We fell in love with a vision and cared enough about it to find the courage to put up with considerable hardship, especially in our early years of teaching. Ultimately courage is found by those who care; those who love exercise courage they didn't know they had when their beloved is endangered. The touchstone of how much we care about the distinctives of Christian higher education will be whether we can find the courage to initiate meaningful reforms.

Money problems we always have with us. Money is a problem right now for most Christian colleges; it will be a problem for those colleges in the future. For some reason money is not a problem for everyone. Some religious leaders have been known to be able to afford five thousand dollar air-conditioned doghouses without skipping meals, but no one has yet discovered how to get the Christian public to support Christian higher education in anything like the same way it supports TV evangelists (though Oral Roberts came close). Christian colleges don't need the scandals and poor taste of some of the media religious figures, but they do remind us of the economic power of the Christian public. Perhaps what we need to do is to find a way to romanticize the academic enterprise, much like missionary work was romanticized in the earlier part of this century. The key is to capture the imaginations of the Christian public. This is fraught with pitfalls, but perhaps someone with creativity and vision can see how to do it. Meanwhile we must be good stewards of what we have. To be a good steward requires keeping our priorities straight.

The proposals in this slim volume seem to us to be reasonable implications of the distinctive goals we have reiterated *ad nauseam*. They are in no imaginable sense intended to be either inclusive or exhaustive. We have often feared that we have been inexcusably timid or blind to exciting possibilities in our suggestions. We hereby give full license to any comers to create striking new designs for the future of Christian higher education. The cost of this license, however, is a caring commitment to those features that render Christian education distinct. Reform is justified only by a radical allegiance to the priorities by which we live as Christian educators.